Acclaim for

Panic No More: Your Guide to Overcome Panic Attacks

Jean Carlton's ***Panic No More*** is an excellent self-help book for patients and therapists. Using her proven techniques can add to the skills of the therapist and can serve as a reassuring guide for the patient. Jean has the unique skill of providing cold data in a warm and very readable style. This book says to the large population of persons who experience panic and phobia conditions that you can seek professional help and your symptoms will be respected in an atmosphere which is caring and supportive while you grow, learn and change.

—Sarah Allison, Ph.D.
Oklahoma Psychological Association Progress Notes

"I want to thank you for writing a great book. ***Panic No More*** has given me a much better understanding of my own problem with panic attacks. I now feel like there is something I can do about the anxiety I've suffered for many years. It is because of your book that I am finally taking action to deal with my panic."

—Gary J.
New York City

Panic No More is a godsend. This book has helped and guided me to emotional, spiritual and physical health on my journey to self-discovery. I could not be where I am today - peaceful - without following Jean's advice.

—Vern W.
Tulsa

PANIC NO MORE

YOUR GUIDE TO OVERCOME PANIC ATTACKS

Jean Carlton

Stonehorse Press
Tulsa, Oklahoma

Stonehorse Press
P.O. Box 701595
Tulsa, Oklahoma 74170

Design cover by Dennis Teutschel
Manufactured in the United States of America
10 9 8 7 6 5 4 3 2

Library of Congress Catalog Card Number: 93-87372

ISBN: 0-9639632-9-5

The author of this book does not dispense medical advice nor prescribe the use of any technique as a form of treatment for physical or medical problems without the advice of a physician, either directly or indirectly. The sole intent of the author is to offer information to help you in your quest for health and well being. In the event you use any of the information in this book for yourself, which is your constitutional right, the author and the publisher assume no responsibility for your actions.

With love,
to my son, John

ATTENTION: SCHOOLS AND INSTITUTIONS

Stonehorse Press books are available at quantity discounts with bulk purchase for educational, business or sales promotional use. For information, please write or call: **Stonehorse Press**, P.O. Box 701595, Tulsa, Oklahoma 74170. (918) 488-9530.

ARE THERE STONEHORSE BOOKS YOU WANT BUT CANNOT FIND IN YOUR LOCAL STORES?

You can get any **Stonehorse Press** book in print. Simply send title and retail price. Oklahoma residents please add 7 1/2 % (97cents) sales tax. Please allow $1.05 for postage and surface shipping. Enclose check or money order to: **Stonehorse Press**, P.O. Box 701595, Tulsa, Oklahoma 74170, or send for our complete catalogue. Order form on page 279.

Jean Carlton is a noted lecturer and licensed psychotherapist in private practice in Tulsa, Oklahoma

CONTENTS

ACKNOWLEDGMENTS

I am greatly indebted to the many people who have helped me along the path. I am especially grateful to Clif Warren and Lynet Wert for teaching me the fundamentals of writing and to Barbara Bartocci who read and reread my manuscript, edited and generally gave me unlimited support. Also, I'm grateful to Janet Rains who allowed me to come to her home, sometimes in the middle of the night, and call her at all times of the day and night with ideas and asking for advice and how to spell certain words. I appreciate all her efforts to read and reread my manuscript in all stages and giving me helpful hints and suggestions. Jan Alan let me stay at her house at a moments notice when I needed to travel to Oklahoma City and helped critique the manuscript. Mary Atwood went with me to seminars and conventions to learn new information, shared her knowledge about spirit healing and introduced me to people who would help me along my path. Many thanks to Jeanie Lovelady for her support and proofing the manuscript. Veronica Winkler lent her unlimited support and her profound gifts of spiritual communication, advice and suggestions for the book. Thanks to Gary Mitchell for his valuable advice and Bill Dodson who taught me more about the effects and treatment of abuse, chemical dependency and narcissism. David Speigel helped enormously with his advise and expertise on medication. Dale Walters for all the biofeedback and hypnosis seminars at the Menninger Foundation.

I wish to thank LeRoy Zemke for making me aware of the light and the spiritual connectedness of all living things. Several of the guided visualizations mentioned in this book are ones he taught me. I give a special thanks to my teacher John Bradshaw who opened a new dimension to my education when I attended the Healing Child seminar in Aspen. Various techniques given in this book come from what I learned from him. Thanks Jerry Densow, who spent many years teaching me meditation and Jean Houston for all the workshops and lectures and her brilliance. And, I wish to thank my departed teachers, Audle Allison and Yogananda.

I also wish to thank my clients over the years for sharing their lives with me. All "stories" have been disguised to protect their confidentiality. Not only have names been changed, but in many instances the sex of the client has also been changed, along with combining stories from several different people. In some cases, the stories have been created to teach the reader how certain situations can affect the psyche.

Many of the ideas in this book are ancient and come from many, many sources. I have not always been able to remember where or from whom I first heard them. My apologies and thanks to anyone whose work may not have been explicitly credited.

INTRODUCTION

Inspiration for this book has come to me on numerous levels. During the past twenty years I have noticed a particular need for an informative book on panic attacks. Most people are unaware of what is happening to them when they have panic attacks. Some seek medical help, only to go from doctor to doctor with no success. Research shows that the average person goes to ten doctors over a period of ten years before they are correctly diagnosed. Many doctors are unfamiliar with panic attack symptoms. They run numerous, very expensive tests, only to find that nothing physically is wrong.

It seemed that approximately eighty per cent of the people I saw, both in private practice and in psychiatric hospitals, had a history of either sexual or physical abuse, as well as panic attacks.

When patients were put on medication, they seemed to stop the process of healing, and rely primarily on the drug to do it for them. I met people who had suffered from panic attacks for over twenty years at a hospital where I worked.

These patients thought that all they could do was take drugs. Some became addicted to them. There seemed to be a connection between sexual abuse or other trauma and panic attacks. This connection has been confirmed over and over again.

When I researched panic attacks, I discovered ten million people suffered from them. Of those ten million, approximately ten per cent of them, had a panic attack when they stepped out in front of an oncoming truck or a similar situation. They dismissed it as stress, and probably didn't have anymore. This situational panic can trigger more attacks in those that worry about them.

INTRODUCTION

New research is beginning to show panic attacks are common symptoms when coping defenses fail. People who move frequently are now known to develop panic attacks. Other situational triggers include divorce, death, financial problems, and multiple operations, to name a few.

It is for people who worry about having panic attacks and allow fear to dominate their life that I have written this book. This book is intended to show a path out of the fear, into the fullness of life.

Once I decided to write this book, all sorts of people began to relate to me their experiences of panic attacks. Some had hidden them from others thinking they were weird, and had never sought help before.

Panic attacks are symptoms of deeper problems. That is why it's important to realize medicating the panic attack does not address the problem. The root of the problem needs healing. *Regardless of the pain, it can be healed.*

We heal by bringing back the fullness of ourselves. Through remembering and re-experiencing our pain, our struggles, our traumas and triumphs we are able to let the pain go. But panic attacks can also occur when aspects of ourselves are denied. The attack then becomes a signal that there is more to the self, more to be discovered than what is encapsulated in a limited identity.

One of the panic attack victim's biggest struggles is to learn to express his or her feelings, and not suppress or repress them; to release their crippling dependency; accept the fullness of their life; become assertive and take action. In a sense, the pain leads the way to fullness and wholeness. Embrace it. Welcome it. Do not run from it. It will lead you into your healing.

CHAPTER 1

PANIC !

Picture yourself. You've just finished working. You pick your child up from day care. You go to the store for a few groceries before going home. You reach for a loaf of bread, and a panic attack strikes. You're short of breath. Your heart starts beating wildly. You feel pressure in your chest. On top of all these things, you feel incredible fear, as if you're suddenly going to die. You just have to get out of there!

You drop the bread, leave the cart, grab your kid's hand and run out of the store. You take a deep breath, and in a few minutes it passes. It's probably one of the most frightening things that's ever happened to you. You hope it won't happen again. But you find yourself thinking about it. You find yourself wondering as you go for groceries the next time, *is this going to happen again?*

And sure enough it does. This time you're at work; in your office. It happens again; the shortness of breath, the pressure in the chest. You may feel dizzy. When you look around, everything is blurred in a haze of bright light. You hear a loud buzzing sound in your ears. You may feel outside of your body. Your body is feeling unreal. Your skin is tingling and your legs feel numb. Your co-workers see you. You look like a ghost. You sit for a few minutes. It gets worse. Your stomach spasms. Your heart races faster. You hit 911 and go to the emergency room.

By this time, you're certain you've had a heart attack; you're scared; you think you're going to *die*! You have an electrocardiogram and blood work done. Everything's fine.

Now you start to have what's called "anticipatory anxiety." You really worry. Can this happen to me again? *When*? You get nervous and worry, "What if this happens while I'm driving?" Not only does a panic attack produce fear, it's embarrassing to leave suddenly from wherever you are. The panic attacks continue. Maybe not so frequently, but enough that your overriding thought becomes, "I hope it won't happen again."

You start going to doctors. Seventy-five per cent of people with panic attacks see ten doctors over ten years before the correct diagnosis is made. Seven hundred thousand cardiac catheterizations a year are done in this country. Two hundred thousand of the patients have normal coronary arteries! Roughly thirty per cent of these, or seventy thousand cardiac catherizations, take place because of panic attacks. It isn't possible to determine if the pain is cardiac or something else until you have the test run.

Half of the angiograms, at $2,000 each, are due to panic attacks each year. In a study done at a university hospital clinic, twenty-three per cent of the people who went to the neurology clinic had panic disorder and no neurological problems.

The large number of people with undiagnosed and untreated panic attacks has led the National Institute of Mental Health to establish a hotline. You can reach it by calling 1-800-64-PANIC.

You visit an ENT specialist, thinking "I was dizzy, maybe it's an inner ear problem." But that doctor tells you nothing's wrong. Then you see a generalist who tells you to see a psychiatrist because your panic is stress related. Then you think, "I wasn't under any stress the day it started. Nothing particular was happening." You just can't explain it.

Panic attacks are an extremely baffling condition. Baffling because it's hard to explain just how frightening it is. It's estimated that two and one half million people in the United States suffer from panic disorder, and ten million people suffer from panic attacks. The number of people who suffer from anxiety is even higher.

Anxiety is simply worrying about what may happen. A panic attack consists of a time frame of approximately ten to twenty minutes where the central nervous system gets out of kilter and causes short circuiting in all parts of the body. A panic disorder occurs when panic attacks continue over a period of a month, and you worry about having more.

The one thing that separates panic attacks from any other type of illness is the overwhelming fear that something dreadful is about to happen. You may feel death is imminent.

After a panic attack, you may think, "it happened to me in that particular store" and decide you won't go to that store again.

"Maybe the store triggered it. Is there something in the air? It happened in a meeting at work too." So you avoid meetings at work. You begin to avoid all shops and meeting rooms.

You take the stairs instead of the elevator and avoid enclosed places, like a theater, where you can't get out quickly in case of a panic attack. You stop driving at night, because what if this happens on the road?

Gradually, your world constricts and contracts. You start avoidance behavior. You refuse to do things alone or in enclosed situations like a movie theater. You may become depressed. You may begin using alcohol or prescription drugs to control panic attacks. Suicide may even seem like a way out. Suicide is most often attempted by those addicted to prescription drugs or alcohol.

You may develop phobias and agoraphobia. Agoraphobia means the abnormal fear of being in an open space. In agoraphobia, you focus on places or situations from which you feel escape might be difficult or embarrassing. You worry that help might not be readily available if you feel trapped. Examples include traveling away from home, being in a crowd, standing in a line, crossing a bridge, or using public transportation. You won't leave your house. You're afraid to step out of the door for fear of having a panic attack. Some people don't go outside their house for more than ten years.

Panic attacks aren't something that's "all in your head." Panic attacks are a significant medical and psychiatric illness that's extremely painful and debilitating.

PANIC ATTACK MIMICS

If you suffer from panic attacks, it is important to get a complete history and physical examination. The reason is to look for other diseases that mimic panic attacks.

PANIC

Diagnosing panic attacks is, in part, a diagnosis of exclusion. You and your doctor need to be certain that no other diseases are producing the panic attack symptoms.

- Hypoglycemia symptoms are very similar to those of panic attacks. Hypoglycemia is caused by an abnormally diminished content of glucose in the blood.
- Hyperthyroidism causes very similar symptoms too. Hyperthyroidism is caused by the excessive functional activity of the thyroid gland. Some people who have shortness of breath and palpitations from hyperthroidism also develop avoidance behavior.
- Hypoxia, lack of oxygen to the brain, occurring in asthma and emphysema, also cause fear and a feeling of impending doom.
- Cardiac disease may mimic panic attack symptoms.
- Temporal lobe epilepsy has similar symptoms.
- Some tumors produce substances that cause constriction of the blood vessels and shortness of breath.

FLIGHT OR FLIGHT

In a panic attack, the body's normal response goes awry. The sympathetic nervous system, which goes throughout the body is responsible for the *fight or flight* response. That means when you're in a situation that is stressful and you have to get away, you breathe faster and your heart beats faster.

This might occur in an attack situation where you have to escape, or when you step out in front of an oncoming truck. You get superhuman strength. This system triggers your survival instincts. But in people prone to panic attacks, this *fight or flight* response also triggers in nonstressful situations, and at random. Panic attacks appear to strike without warning.

Most people who have panic attacks feel they last for hours and hours, because the pain seems to last forever. Current research shows that a panic attack peaks within the first ten and may continue another ten minutes. The anxiety may take several hours to come down from after the attack. That's how long it takes the adrenaline to dissipate from the body. But the fear may last and cause you to worry about losing control again.

WHO HAS PANIC ATTACKS

Women between the ages of twenty and forty-five are most prone to having panic attacks. Men also have panic attacks, but often cover it up by drinking. Children who become fearful of going to school are usually diagnosed as suffering from separation anxiety, but may be having panic attacks. Older people, age sixty-five or more can also have panic attacks.

There is an increased rate of depression and suicide in people who have panic attacks. Thirty per cent of people with panic disorder have a serious bout with depression. A very significant number of people become alcoholic trying to relieve the symptoms of panic attacks.

PANIC ATTACKS EASILY TREATED

Panic attacks are easily treated by a combination of different therapies, such as behavior modification, exposure therapy, relaxation therapy, cognitive therapy, psychotherapy, and biofeedback. Behavior modification helps identify situations that are triggers for panic attacks and teaches you how to overcome them. It is most often used when people have avoidance behavior and are afraid to drive a car.

PANIC

Keri was twenty-two when she and her husband divorced, leaving her alone to provide for their two year old son. She developed panic attacks and became afraid to drive her car. She had to depend on other people for rides. After the appropriate behavior modification treatment, she was able to drive her car again. Panic attacks are very treatable. Psychotherapy works well for depression and panic attacks. If there is a problem with alcohol, chemical dependency treatment is necessary.

MEDICATION

Most people, unaware they're having panic attacks, complain of physical discomfort when they go to the doctor. They talk about the abdominal distress or the racing, pounding heart. Many doctors are unfamiliar with panic attack symptoms, and the diagnosis is missed much of the time. Some people go to as many as ten doctors before the correct diagnosis is made.

The Federal Drug and Food Administration has approved only one drug for the treatment of panic—Xanax. It is immediately effective, but can be highly addictive if you have a history of drug or alcohol abuse or if you are the child of an alcoholic. It may need to be administered three to six times daily. It is also difficult to get off. Tapering down the dose slowly for weeks is the best way to stop and avoid withdrawal.

There are four other groups of drugs that are effective and prescribed for the treatment of panic even though only one has been approved.

1. Tricyclic antidepressants, including:

Brand Name	**Generic Name**
• Anafranil	• clomipramine
• Tofranil	• imipramine

• Elavil	• amitriptyline
• Aventyl	• nortriptyline
• Asendin	• amoxapine
• Sinequan	• doxepin

The problem with these drugs is that they all have side effects: dry mouth, constipation, drowsiness, and sometimes when the medications are first started, they induce panic attacks. They take time to work—three, four, five to six weeks.

2. Monoamine Oxidase (MAOI) inhibitors include:

Brand Name	**Generic Name**
• Nardil	• phenelzine
• Marplan	• isocarboxazid
• Parnate	• tranylcypromine

These drugs are effective in panic disorder. They also treat depression and avoidance behavior. You need to be on a very strict diet, and avoid cheese, wine, and things like sour cream, beer, red wines, ripe bananas, and meat. These drugs can cause serious physical problems such as high blood pressure, severe headaches and even death if you eat the wrong foods.

3. Benzodiazepines including:

Name Brand	**Generic Brand**
• Librium	• chlordiazepoxide
• Tranxene	• clorazepate
• Valium	• diazepam
• Clonopin	• clonazepam
• Xanax	• alprazolam
• Paxipam	• halazepam
• Halcion	• triazolam
• Dalmane	• flurazepam
• Centrax	• prazepam

• Restoril	• temazepam
• Serax	• oxazepam
• Ativan	• lorazepam

The advantage to these medications is that they work immediately. The disadvantage is their addictive quality. They can also cause depression. Some are very sedating and act as a disinhibitor. That means if you are depressed and think about suicide, you may actually try it because your inhibitions are lowered. For this reason these drugs are not a first choice. They may cause memory disturbance or drowsiness. It may be necessary to administer them three to six times daily because of their short acting nature.

4. SRRI Serotonin uptake inhibitors including:

Name Brand	**Generic Name**
• Prozac	• fluoxetine
• Zoloft	• sertraline

The problem with these drugs is that they can cause excitability and anxiety. Some can even cause panic attacks.

Drugs that have not been researched thoroughly to determine their overall effectiveness, but are probably effective include:

Brand Name	**Generic Name**
• Norpramin	• desipramine
• Prozac	• fluoxetine
• Pamelor	• nortriptyline
• Elavil	• amitriptyline
• Sinequan	• doxepin

Drugs not effective for panic attacks include:

Brand Name	**Generic Name**
• Busepar	• buspirone
• Inderal, a beta blocker	• propranolol

Symptoms of withdrawal from drugs frequently overlap with anxiety symptoms, so when you try and get off the drug, symptoms return. You might think it's relaspe when it's only withdrawal. Actual relaspe usually occurs within the first three months after you stop taking the drug if no other form of therapy is given. Tapering off the drug slowly helps avoid relaspe.

It's not necessary to use drugs to overcome panic attacks. Some of the drugs prescribed to control panic attacks can actually cause them, in addition to the numerous side effects like depression, dry mouth, nausea and diarrhea. Prescription drugs can cause psychological addiction if you use them to cope with uncomfortable feelings or situations—and that's what you're taking them for! Some of the drugs prescribed for panic attacks are highly chemically addictive. Some have a toxic effect, especially if you are pregnant. There is no long term gain using drugs unless some form of therapy—behavior modification, cognitive therapy, psychotherapy or other form of therapy is also utilized. Drugs don't teach you problem solving or coping skills.

If the drug stops the panic attacks, they can start again when you stop taking them. The underlying self-image and role of a sick person, or helpless victim hasn't had time to change. When you get overwhelmed, you might panic.

Therapy is important to assist you in resolving these issues besides addressing the underlying problems that cause panic attacks. The kinds of techniques discussed in this book are ones that I have found effective for over twenty years in treating panic attack victims. When my methods that treat the body, mind, and spirit are used, the effects are not only long lasting, they are transforming.

CHAPTER 2

WHO HAS PANIC ATTACKS?

Panic attack victims frequently describe a parent who is strict, cold and harsh in attitude. That kind of parent stifles you in your own ideas and creativity. You get punished for doing things on your own and become intimidated into passivity. Controlled and manipulated by guilt and shame, you then seek the parent's approval to avoid those feelings. You avoid conflict type situations all together, because it's safer.

Ironically, blind obedience to adults makes you a possible target for sexual abuse. The inability to say "No" leaves you with no self-defense.

If you get molested, you may feel guilty and hide what happened. Those painful memories and feelings are usually repressed in childhood. But they erupt later in life, creating sick and crazy feelings, and panic attacks. When you reach the age of twenty-one or twenty-two, the image of your parent becomes a part of your own psyche. Your parent's voice now echoes inside your head. It puts you down, chastises and ridicules you.

This causes non-assertive, fearful, anxious feelings and behavior. You seek approval, and protection from this internal persecution, by attaching yourself to an authority figure, friend, or spouse. But the relationship eventually becomes one of crippling dependency.

When repression occurs in childhood, you may grow up sexually inhibited and numb on the inside. You may feel embarrassment and shame about sexuality. You may not have the faintest idea how to express or talk about feelings, or have a feeling vocabulary. You strive to look good on the outside, become successful, but inside you feel inadequate and hold everything in.

You're like a volcano, building up pressure with pent up emotions. Then an internal explosion occurs and causes a panic attack.

Many people suffer attacks during sleep. These may occur along with nightmares, about one to two hours after they fall asleep. The electrical storm short circuits various parts of your body. You may wake up feeling suffocated. Your heart may race and pound, and at the same time, your body jerks uncontrollably. Some people never develop a full blown panic disorder, but have panic attacks in their sleep every so often.

Relaxation and proper breathing techniques are very helpfu in reducing panic attacks. A simple test to determine where you are breathing is to place one hand on your chest and one hand on your abdomen. Which hand moves? People who are anxious and fearful breathe high in their chest. When they gasp for air, a process called reverse thoracic breathing begins. These light, shallow, rapid breaths are called hyperventilation.

HYPERVENTILATION

Hyperventilation is the basis of the primitive *fight or flight* mechanism. It pushes all the alarm buttons in the body. Our brain has not changed since the days of the caveman, but our society and culture have. Your boss threatens your job and the *fight or flight* response gets triggered. Your heart pounds out of control and engorge the blood vessels.

In this hypervigilant state you automatically scan the environment for danger, to fight or flee from it. You shake and tremble, but there's nowhere to run. This primitive response triggers an adrenaline surge. The blood draws away from the extremities and centers around the heart area and in the large muscles. Our caveman ancestors needed this response to fight wild animals. The blood around the heart insured survival. The large muscles have added strength to run.

Digestion shuts down and the blood is suddenly capable of clotting faster. Once the *flight or fight* response is triggered, it takes fifteen to forty-five minutes for the body to return to normal. Uncontrolled hyperventilation can be crippling and sometimes life-threatening. The brain becomes depleted of oxygen. The lack of oxygen in the brain triggers an instinctual fear of impending doom and death. You suddenly feel overwhelming fear and panic.

The cardiovascular system effects palpitations, missing heartbeats, chest pain and Raynaud's disease, a deadening of the fingers and toes. It can destabilize the central nervous system and cause dizziness, disturbances of vision and tingling sensations or numbness.

Learning to redirect yourself to do regular, even, continuous diaphragm breathing stops many of the limited symptoms and panic attacks. To make regular, even, breaths, count to five breathing in, and count to five breathing out. Hyperventilation depletes the balance of oxygen in the body. This breathing exercise rebalances the oxygen.

To practice diaphragm breathing, lie flat on your back and place a book on your abdomen. Shift your breathing deeper and further down in your body until the book begins to rise and fall as you breathe. Then you're breathing correctly.

If you've done reverse thoracic breathing any length of time, proper, deep diaphragm breathing may feel very strange. Remind yourself over and over to pay attention to your breath and redirect yourself in a kind, gentle manner to slow down and breathe from the diaphragm.

DYSFUNCTIONAL BELIEFS

Misinformation and dysfunction handed down through your family may place you at risk for developing panic disorder. The correct information about what is, and is not, harmful to your body is important knowledge.

Beliefs play a big role in determining how you react to situations. Some people believe anxiety symptoms have harmful consequences. These beliefs create a hypersensitivity to anxiety. People with high anxiety sensitivity may misinterpret a rapid heart rate as an impending heart attack. But people with low anxiety sensitivity regard the same symptom as stress.

ANXIETY SENSITIVITY

If you are anxiety sensitive, you believe that anxiety can cause illness, and you worry about the possibility of becoming anxious. You tend to avoid situations where you might get anxious. If you believe that anxiety causes heart attacks you will be more anxious than if you don't share this belief.

The Anxiety Rating Scale included below has sixteen items specifying a possible negative consequence to the experience of anxiety. These consequences include additional anxiety or fear, illness, embarrassment, and loss of control.

Rate each item by selecting one of five phrases. The phrases are, very little (scored as 0 points), a little (1 point), some (2 points), much (3 points) and very much (4 points). Your anxiety score is the sum of the scores on the sixteen items. The ARS only measures anxiety sensitivity; not anxiety.

ANXIETY RATING SCALE (ARS)

ITEM	SCORE
1. It scares me when I am anxious.	( )
2. When I notice that my heart beats fast or irregularly, I worry that I might have a heart attack.	( )
3. It scares me when I feel I might lose control.	( )
4. When my mind wanders, I worry that I might be going crazy.	( )
5. It scares me when I have to write a check in public.	( )
6. It is important to me not to appear anxious.	( )
7. I worry about becoming seriously ill.	( )
8. It scares me when my hands shake.	( )

9. It embarrasses me when my body makes sounds. ( )
10. It scares me when I can't breathe easily. ( )
11. It's important to me to stay in control of my feelings. ( )
12. It scares me when I can't concentrate. ( )
13. Other people notice when I feel nervous. ( )
14. Unusual body sensations frighten me. ( )
15. When I am nervous, I worry that I might go crazy. ( )
16. It scares me when I feel sick. ( )

Normal subjects score about 18.4. People with panic disorder, with or without agoraphobia, typically score in the mid-thirties. Agoraphobia, the *fear of fear,* is discussed in Chapter 10. Agoraphobics generally score higher than other anxiety disorders, and those with anxiety disorders score higher than normal subjects.

Anxiety sensitivity may be a predisposing factor in the development of fears and panic attacks. Belief that anxiety has few or no negative effects, enables you to cope with higher levels of anxiety. In contrast if you believe that anxiety has terrible effects, such as heart attacks and mental illness, you may have anxiety reactions that grow in anticipation of severe consequences. When you experience the symptoms you believe to have harmful consequences, you may panic.

Studies show people with high anxiety sensitivity seek treatment more frequently and report more first-degree relatives with a history of panic, than those who score low on the ARS.

MARGARET

Margaret is in her seventies. She has no children. She got along fine until her husband died. They had been very close, and he pampered her. Margaret had never spent a night alone in her life. After his death, she became fearful at night. A niece by marriage volunteered to stay with her for awhile.

Margaret's home is worth several million dollars. Her niece, realizing Margaret's mental condition, began to capitalize on her fears. She moved into the home and catered to Margaret. She bathed and lotioned her skin.

She told Margaret she loved to take care of her, and that she would prepare meals and do shopping. Margaret became increasingly dependent upon her niece and thought she couldn't live without her. The niece constantly undermined Margaret by insinuating she would die soon and join her husband. Although Margaret was quite healthy, she believed her.

Then, her niece threatened to leave her alone to die if she didn't sign the house over. Margaret panicked and signed part of it over to her. The niece had a will made out in which Margaret left everything to her, and she signed that too. Then the niece stopped tending to her needs. She did things to frighten and intimidate Margaret.

Margaret became so terrified that her muscles knotted up all over her body. Her skin burned and itched constantly. She couldn't relax. She was afraid to say anything which might make her niece angry. So, she kept quiet, and her muscles knotted up more. Margaret complained of loneliness, and her niece told her no one wanted to be with her. She shut her away in her room.

Margaret called several doctors, complaining of her skin burning and itching. One told her to gain weight. He said she didn't have enough meat on her to cover her nerves. Another gave her pills. Margaret became afraid of what might happen to her.

Margaret came to see me, and asked to be hypnotized in order to be made unafraid of her niece. After assessing the situation, I treated Margaret with psychotherapy for insight, and used hand-warming biofeedback and guided visualizations to help her relax. She learned how to control and relax her body and her burning, itching skin sensations decreased. After Margaret verbalized her fears and anxieties, she discovered new confidence in her self, and put her life in order. She's beginning to see her niece for what she is. Margaret is consulting a lawyer and making out a new will. She's also learning she is okay alone.

CHAPTER 3

WHERE ARE YOUR FEELINGS

Underlying psychological problems and lack of coping skills are typical of people who develop panic attacks. Pent up feelings often trigger attacks in sensitive people.

You may feel so programmed with expectations of the way life *should* be, that you're not sure what your real feelings are. These bottled up feelings, fears and frustrations may make you feel out of control.

Expectations are difficult to define because they are accepted as the way life is. If you're expected to get married and have children, you may not have developed enough of an individual identity to have a successful marriage. How can you relate in an intimate relationship when you don't even know who you are as a person?

Dysfunctional families condition family members to all think alike, feel the same way, and mesh their identities. Individuality is discouraged. If a member rebels and does his own thing, he is regarded as a "black sheep." The dysfunctional family motto is, "Look good on the outside and deny any conflicts or depression you may feel on the inside."

As more families become dysfunctional, the number of people who suffer panic attacks increases. The National Institute of Mental Health estimates as high as ten million people in the United States are now afflicted. Seventy-five per cent of these are women. Before you panic over these statistics, let me tell you the good news. You can overcome panic attacks. I have been counseling people suffering from panic attacks for over twenty years. Most of the people have overcome their fears and all of them have improved the quality of their life. This book describes the successful methods I use.

Women are the hardest hit by panic attacks. Some researchers suspect hormonal imbalances, but this has not been proven. Women are, historically, in a double bind. To be feminine, you emulate the characteristics of being passive, dependent, gentle and nurturing. Women are historically trained to deny strong emotions. Increasing pressures of rearing children in single parent households, job demands, financial strain, and lack of assertiveness skills leave women too vulnerable.

If you are perfectionistic, a high achiever, extremely sensitive, and prone to jump to conclusions, you may trigger panic attacks when you feel overwhelmed. This can happen when your own natural feelings reach the surface and make you feel out of control because you're conditioned to feel the "acceptable ways."

Linda, an attractive thirty-two year old married woman, exuded a happy-go-lucky attitude about life. Whenever a problem came along, she pretended it wasn't there. In her family, people were supposed to look good on the outside and become successful.

In therapy, Linda had trouble identifying her true feelings because she had denied them for so long. Her life had become one endless series of masks. She'd lost touch with her authentic self.

She was very attached to her stepfather, a security figure, and thought he would always be there to take care of her. Even though Linda was married, both she and her husband depended upon her stepfather to relieve their financial stress. His sudden death traumatized her.

By the time she came for counseling, she shook all over, drank heavily, and seemed well on her way to becoming an alcoholic. She used alcohol and prescription drugs to escape the deadly symptoms of her panic attacks. The fear of being alone in the world without the protection of her stepfather terrified her. She didn't know how to solve problems or take care of herself.

She mourned her stepfather and his loss in her life. "Do you think I'll ever stop crying?" she asked, wiping her eyes. "This has always been my worst fear, that if I ever let myself feel, I'd just cry for the rest of my life."

After Linda had cried for awhile, I said, "It's not just Walter's dying. The tears are about all the disappointments in your life."

"I know that," her lower lip quivered as she spoke. "I just pretended I was happy. That's what people expected of me, and I gave it to them." During the following weeks, Linda relived sad incidents that had happened in her life.

"I remember when my parents divorced. It was just awful. My mother came into my bedroom and said she and my father were getting a divorce and that he was leaving. I was only thirteen. I didn't know what to do. Nothing was ever said again. No one in my family ever talked about problems. They didn't exist. We all pretended everything was all right."

As she began to cry again, she looked like a very young, very hurt child. "I had to move out of our nice big house, and leave all my friends, and the neighborhood I knew. We moved across town into a little place, and I was ashamed of it.

My whole life changed at that point, and I couldn't even discuss it. I just went on manufacturing "happy" feelings because that's what people wanted from me. And now it's all catching up with me . . . all the pain."

As her face turned pale, she started to hyperventilate. "Oh, no. It's happening again. See," she said, holding out her shaking hands, "I'm out of control now."

"You've been having panic attacks and here's what you can do to overcome them. Shift your breathing down to your abdomen and take slow, deep diaphragm breaths. For right now, visualize a figure eight, and trace it with the in breath and the out breath, making it continuous." Linda's stomach was shaking so much she had to stand up and unzip her jeans in order to increase her breathing.

"I thought I was supposed to breathe up in my chest and have a flat stomach," she chattered nervously. "Do you mean I need to breathe deeper? What about the military? Don't they teach you to stick your chest out and suck in your stomach? I'll have to start wearing looser clothing. I could never take a deep breath in these tight jeans."

Linda's series of unending questions were a lot like the way she handles her life. She rambled on jumping from topic to topic without giving herself time to process her own thoughts.

"For now, focus on your breathing. Slow it down, take even, continuous breaths," I said. "It's easier if you wear clothes you can breathe in. Tight designer jeans force you to hyperventilate."

Linda learned to regulate her breathing, and take slow, continuous, deep diaphragm breaths. Her panic attacks became less frequent, and finally stopped. Her binge drinking also stopped. She limited herself to a glass of wine at night. Through therapy, she learned to accept the pain and disappointments which come in life. Linda began to have genuine "bright sunshiny days" full of joy.

PANIC ATTACK SYMPTOMS

The more you know about panic attacks, the better your chances are at overcoming them. Panic attack symptoms vary from individual to individual and appear to strike without warning. Attacks consist of a period of intense fear and discomfort, with abrupt onset of at least four of the following symptoms:

- faintness, dizziness or unsteadiness
- hyperventilation
- tremor
- choking
- inability to swallow
- lump in the throat
- racing, pounding, skipping heartbeats
- sweating, burning, itching, or tingling skin
- nausea
- chills or flushing
- derealization
- fear of dying

- fear of going crazy or losing control
- abdominal distress
- numbness
- shortness of breath or smothering feeling
- trembling or shaking

If a sensitive person who has panic attacks doesn't find out how to stop them, the frequency, fear and worry lead to the development of a panic disorder. One or more panic attacks within a month, and the fear or worry of having more attacks which causes altered behavior, (avoidance behavior) signals a panic disorder.

This is a very serious condition, and you may unknowingly trigger attacks by thinking about them. Persistent fears of having attacks may cause you to feel helpless and obsess about having a mysterious disease to explain what's happening to you. You might avoid places for fear of having an attack. This can eventually lead to developing phobias about situations or places where attacks occurred. The resulting despair may lead to impulsive suicide attempts just to get relief from the pain.

Not everyone who has panic attacks or a limited symptom develops a panic disorder. If you think a pounding heart signals an impending heart attack, and take your symptoms seriously, your chances are higher for developing a panic disorder than someone who dismisses it as a sign of stress.

Since panic attack symptoms mimic those of cardiac, endocrine, and convulsive disorders, victims often go to their physician or race to a hospital emergency room. You may be misdiagnosed or have coexisting medical conditions. The *Archives of Internal Medicine* reports fifty-nine per cent of the patients attending a cardiology clinic with atypical chest pain and no arteriographic evidence of coronary artery disease were found to have panic disorder.

GEORGE

Five people died in George's family in less than a year. He wondered if he was next. He had trouble breathing. He felt suffocated. His blood pressure measured at stroke level, while his heart pounded out of control. He thought he was having a heart attack, but at the hospital emergency room, they sent George to the psychiatric unit. Doctors treated George with a hypertensive medication, along with individual and group psychotherapy. During therapy he struggled to express his feelings.

George put his hands over his heart, "I'll never tell anyone what I feel inside. It's just too awful," he said. "Never." As he gained in trust, his story came out amidst tears of sorrow. He felt overwhelmed with guilt, remorse, and grief about his wife's death. For over a year, he had watched helplessly as she died of cancer. When they were younger, they put off going places, and saved their money. They'd talked about traveling "someday." Now, he had the money to do what they dreamed of . . . but she was gone. But there was more.

Before her death, his wife chain-smoked and drank alone. He hid her problems from friends and relatives. George felt hurt and anger at his wife for not being more available when she was alive. He tried to deny the feelings, but soon the burden of protecting her image crumbled. Finally, he accepted his pain and anger.

George knew very little about taking care of himself, such as buying groceries, or taking care of the house. After his wife's death, he went home at the end of each work day and stared at the walls. During his two weeks stay at the hospital, and subsequently at his aftercare therapy sessions, George learned to take care of himself.

He made a "feelings sheet" of words he needed to work on to identify his feelings. He also learned how to prepare meals and run the vacuum sweeper.

He started an exercise program and lost weight. As his appearance and attitude changed, he found several women who were interested in him. He grieved for his deceased wife, but put the past in the past. Then he started to enjoy the present.

ADDICTION TO ALCOHOL AND DRUGS

Many panic attack victims become addicted to alcohol and prescription drugs trying to suppress their feelings and their symptoms.

Alcohol is the quickest way to stop a panic attack. For that reason, many people who have panic attacks carry a flask of whiskey. They take a drink whenever they feel an attack starting.

This attempt at self-medication often leads to addiction. Alcoholism is a subtle disease. It starts slowly. But, over a period of time, the ingestion of alcohol to numb feelings and make you comfortable and less inhibited in situations takes its toll.

It starts producing a substance in the brain known as THIQ (tetrahydroisoquinoline). Once the brain starts producing THIQ, you're addicted.

Some types of alcoholism can be inherited. If you have one parent or grandparent who was alcoholic, your chances of developing alcoholism are fifty per cent. If you have two parents or grandparents who are alcoholic, your chances of developing alcoholism are eighty per cent. Chemical dependency can also develop if you drink or use prescription drugs to cope with feelings or unpleasant situations. Anyone can become addicted if the addictive substance is taken frequently enough over a period of time. And some prescription drugs are highly addictive, even some of the ones prescribed for panic attacks.

MARLA

When Marla realized she didn't provide adequate care for her small children, she entered chemical dependency treatment. She had frequently called in sick to work due to hangovers and because she wanted to stay home, drink, and avoid people.

Most of her drinking was hidden from her husband. Marla's mother was an alcoholic who stayed home and drank most of her days away. When Marla sobered up at treatment, she learned that she used alcohol to cope with her anxiety. Although Marla was an excellent lawyer, she panicked at the thought of attending professional meetings. She feared someone might think she was a fraud. She also experienced anxiety about appointments with clients and her boss. When Marla left the treatment center she began to work on overcoming her anxiety and panic attacks.

If you have become addicted to alcohol as a result of attempting to cope with panic attacks, you must first stop drinking and go through withdrawal from alcohol. For some, going to Alcoholics Anonymous meetings and working the twelve steps is enough. Others may need to enter a chemical dependency treatment center. But you must stop drinking before you can expect to get better. Once THIQ is produced in the brain, you can never drink again.

Statistically, suicide becomes a threat if you use alcohol or drugs to control panic attacks. Twenty per cent of people with panic disorder attempt suicide. The risk increases with drug abuse. The longer you suffer panic attacks, the more helpless and debilitated you may become. Coping skills get strained and often suicide seems the only way out.

The younger you are at the onset of panic disorder, the higher the risk of a suicide attempt. If your first panic attack occurs at age fifteen, you're at higher risk than someone at age thirty-four.

When you're young, you often think you'll feel the same way the rest of your life. You don't understand that your beliefs and thoughts control how you feel. Changing attitudes changes feelings.

When you're young, you don't have the coping skills or know how to solve problems. You are dependent upon parents and frequently don't have the resources to change your situation. You may look for ways to escape. Drugs, alcohol, and suicide are all escapes.

Fourteen year old Lisa came for therapy after taking an overdose of her mother's sleeping pills. During her first session she had a panic attack and hyperventilated until she almost fainted. "It's an unwritten rule at our house," she said. "No one talks about problems. You're the only person who cares about me. I think my mother and father would be happier if I died. They never want to listen to me or my problems." Once Lisa realized it was okay to talk about her family problems, she felt relieved.

"Daddy," she cried during a family session, "you don't realize I took the pills to get your attention. I worked hard in school and made straight A's, just so you'd notice me. But you never did." Her father stared out the window without speaking. Her mother and younger brother and sister looked off in different directions. It was as if no one heard her.

"It sounds like you want a relationship with your father."

"Yes, but look at them," she motioned at her family. "They treat me as if I'm invisible. I laid on the floor dying before anyone ever noticed I was even there."

"Mr. Brandon, is that true?" I asked.

He turned his head slowly and made eye contact with me. "Of course not," he said under his breath.

"Lisa's begging for your attention. Can you look at her?"

He turned his head slightly and nodded at Lisa.

"That's it," Lisa cried. "He rejects me constantly. He doesn't love me, he doesn't want me. He can't even look at me. I might as well be dead."

Mr. Brandon glanced at his wife. "What's the matter with her?"

"She wants your love," his wife said. "Just like the rest of us."

"Mr. Brandon, can you look at Lisa and tell her you care about her? She's very hurt that you don't pay attention to her."

He stared out the window a long time, and then turned to Lisa. "I really do love you," he said looking at her.

"Did you know that's the very first time you ever said " I love you to me?" Lisa said. "I've waited all my life to hear those words from you."

During the following sessions, the entire family became more open and available for each other. When Lisa realized her father didn't have close relationships with anyone in the family, she stopped taking his distancing personally.

Eventually, Lisa healed from feeling emotionally abandoned. She knew she might not always get what she wanted emotionally, but she wasn't afraid to ask for what she needed, including affection from her father.

Lisa started the first teenage suicide hot line and peer suicide counseling at her high school. She enjoyed helping others talk out their problems, instead of trying to escape them.

ONSET OF PANIC ATTACKS

People who develop panic attacks may experience their first symptoms in their teens, late twenties or early thirties. They may continue having symptoms until around the age of fifty-five. This is the time of menopause for most women. During this time many women may have trouble with sexual feelings and issues, problems with untreated sexual abuse, or hormonal imbalances.

People in their late twenties or early thirties face the challenge of taking their place in and with the world. Those who grew up in dysfunctional homes lack coping skills to function adequately. Anxiety may overwhelm them and cause a limited symptom attack when under stress. Panic attacks take place when other coping mechanisms fail.

If you don't get upset about having a panic attack and dismiss it as stress, chances are it won't happen again, or as often. You may need to increase your coping skills by taking classes in assertiveness training. Learning to identify and express your feelings also helps.

HISTORICAL ASPECTS OF PANIC ATTACKS

Panic attacks have been classified by many different names at differing periods in history. The Greeks and Romans called it hysteria. They chose this name because they thought it was primarily a disease effecting the uterus. The word hysteria derives from the Latin, hystericus, and from the Greek words, husterikos, hustera meaning womb.

Religious laws strictly prohibited research of the uterus in Roman and Greek times. Due to their limited knowledge, the Greeks and Romans theorized that the uterus became dislodged from its anatomical location, and wandered around the body. It might wander into the heart area, and cause crowding, which led the heart to race and skip beats. It might also wander into the lung area, crowding the lungs and causing shortness of breath and hyperventilation.

This is the way they explained the many phenomenon of the panic attack symptoms. When a woman aged beyond her child bearing years, providing she survived, the symptoms went away.

Freud's analysis of women of the 19th century revealed many hysterics. He attributed the cause to sexual repression. Not only were women of the 19th century sexually repressed culturally, some were reporting incidents involving actual incest. Freud dismissed these accounts as fantasy.

Cultural mores and values change with the age, but the causes of panic attacks continue to involve repressed feelings, whether they are sexual, or from family dysfunction. Sensitive people who deny their feelings are courting trouble. The subconscious seeks to discharge pent up energy and may trigger a panic attack.

CHAPTER 4

GETTING IN TOUCH WITH YOUR FEELINGS

Martha fidgeted with her purse. "I don't know where to begin," she said. "I feel numb. I have panic attacks a couple of times a year. Then I'm okay for awhile."

Martha looked at the floor, avoiding eye contact. "I have such a hard time talking about my feelings. I stay in my head." Martha's avoidance of her uncomfortable feelings causes her panic attacks.

If your internal feelings are uncomfortable, in conflict, or confused, then you might push them away. All you want is to feel better. You could overeat and symbolically stuff your feelings down, or create crises to distract yourself from distressing internal responses. Just like a cut on your arm throbbing in pain, the pain of panic signals an alarm you need healing. The body knows wholeness. Stuffed feelings eventually turn into panic attacks. You're not whole, and need healing on the mental and emotional planes.

Overcoming repression requires effort. Blocking feelings doesn't mean you're not having them. Because they're blocked, they continue to seek expression, and can cause upset stomachs, headaches, and the complete array of panic attack symptoms.

IDENTIFYING FEELINGS

The first step toward getting in touch with your feelings requires mindfulness of your reactions. The following signs indicate something's going on emotionally which is beyond your immediate awareness:

- the tightness in the chest
- a clenched fist
- gritting your teeth

Even though you may be unaware of your feelings, your body stores memories and the feelings associated with them until they are processed. Tense body muscles reflect repressed unconscious conflicts and feelings. The rigidity of the body posture becomes like armor to contain them.

Relaxation exercises are helpful because a relaxed body is a better barometer to measure tension. If you're "uptight" and tense, it is more difficult to identify your reactions. When you deny your feelings, they get stronger in the unconscious, just like water flowing against a dam. When enough pressure is thrust against the dam, it breaks open, and the water cascades out like a tidal wave. In the same way, feelings explode into consciousness, causing panic attacks.

If you aren't in touch with your feelings, you probably don't have a feeling vocabulary. Once you can name emotions, they're easier to identify and experience.

This list of descriptive words about feelings will help you become familiar with, and identify, emotions.

LOVE, AFFECTION, AND CONCERN

admire	adorable	affectionate	devoted
charitable	benign	giving	care
comforting	friendly	wonderful	generous
cordial	warm	honest	genuine
forgive	tolerant	loving	whole
good	confident	nice	kind
mild	humane	peaceful	sweet
open	helpful	reliable	respectful
polite	patient	truthful	trust
tender			

JOY

amused	enthusiastic	calm	dynamic
comical	terrific	felicity	pleasant
exciting	proud	overjoyed	joyful
glorious	grand	delighted	vital
happy	fit	cheerful	inspired
pleased	vivacious	exalted	excellent
splendid	superb	gay	ecstatic

elevated	fantastic	satisfied	brilliant
enchanted	thrilled	majestic	blissful
glad	happiness	gaiety	pleasure

POTENCY

able	capable	heroic	spirited
brave	firm	powerful	important
daring	sure	potent	bold
energetic	determined	assured	courageous
hardy	sharp	competent	effective
intense	healthy	gallant	strength
secure	fearless	mighty	robust
strong	adequate	skillful	virile

DEPRESSION

abandoned	jilted	alienated	wounded
depressed	despairing	dejected	whipped
destroyed	discarded	despised	pathetic
desolate	gloomy	humiliated	isolated
forlorn	defeated	horrible	glum
guilt	blue	loathed	wrecked
lousy	regretful	miserable	dismal
moody	debased	ruined	dejected

DISTRESS

afflicted	futile	awkward	lost
clumsy	unsure	harrowed	offended
displeased	painful	helpless	nauseated
bother	upset	annoy	vexed
foolish	silly	disturbed	hindered

impaired	troubled	perturbed	skeptical
disliked	puzzled	touchy	grief stricken
doubtful	unsatisfied	sickened	worried

FEAR, ANXIETY

afraid	jittery	scared	tension
bashful	uneasy	nervous	misgiving
fidgety	panicky	strained	trepidation
hesitant	worrying	panic	anxious
on edge	dread	tense	fearful
shaky	alarmed	restless	threatened
timid	churn	jumpy	insecure
jealous	desperate	horrified	scared
shy	frightened	embarrassed	terrified

INADEQUACY

anemic	sickly	insufficient	meek
deficient	defective	wanting	useless
fragile	incompetent	crippled	slight
harmless	exhausted	unfit	unsound
inferior	disabled	powerless	incomplete
shaken	cowardly	small	lacking
unequal	meager	exposed	puny
broken	incapable	vulnerable	inept

ANGER, HOSTILITY

agitated	nasty	angry	irk
arrogant	hard	hostile	resentment
callous	contrary	violent	outrage
cross	biting	bully	fury

fierce	aggressive	annoyed	wrath
mad	belligerent	savage	revenge
severe	vindictive	rage	blunt
wrathful	mean	enraged	harsh
furious	harsh	obstinate	cruel

Using the lists above, make a feeling sheet of the ones you want to work on. If you want to identify anger, stop yourself three times a day and ask, "Today, until this moment, I was angry at ________." If you are working on identifying fear, stop yourself three times a day and ask, "Today, until this moment, I was afraid of ________." Negative emotions are as important to express as positive ones.

Once you can identify those feelings with ease and recognize them, change the list and work on others. Go through the list of emotions until you are comfortable with them. Be patient with yourself. You have all the time you need to do this.

After a few days of working the exercise, you'll recognize specific feelings as you experience them. This exercise is designed to work on the feelings you are least able to identify. When you encounter your feelings, you may think you're out of control, because you're used to suppressing them. Notice your internal dialogue; your thoughts that go over and over in your head. Write them down. Your beliefs and thoughts determine what you feel. Trace your internal dialogue to the feelings they produce. You'll be surprised at the results.

HELEN

Helen, a petite woman in her forties, talked in a sweet, soft, slow, voice. When she started working on anger, she discovered intense anger at her parents. Her session went like this:

Helen: My parents never gave me enough attention. I wanted to be told I was beautiful. I liked to think of myself as a princess, but they treated me with indifference. That's always been a disappointment to me. Nothing I ever did was ever good enough for them. Now, I'm constantly looking for attention from others. No one seems to notice me. I'm so miserable. I think of ways to get even with my parents. It's all their fault. I get panicky when I think I'll never get the attention I crave.

Jean: You sound like you feel you don't exist unless someone notices you. Are you looking to others to validate and affirm you?

Helen: I don't know. All I think about is how to get even with my parents. I want to see them suffer.

Jean: You're hanging on to resentment and revenge and feeling miserable. Your parents can't change the way they treated you in the past, but you can change how you feel about it now.

Helen: Yes, I understand all that. I guess I feel they can still hurt me. I feel helpless where they're concerned. They're never going to give me what I want.

Jean: You may be right about not getting what you want from your parents. But you're about as helpless as a saber toothed tiger. You can give yourself what your parents never did. You can give yourself the nurturing and attention you didn't get from your parents, instead of nursing the old hurts and wounds. Focus away from the pain into the fullness of what you can do for yourself.

Helen: I guess you're right. I'm not really helpless. But someday I might get the chance to get even. I want to be the one responsible for their suffering.

Jean: How will causing them to suffer make you feel better? Isn't that causing you to feel miserable?

Helen: Yes, but they denied me what I had rightfully coming to me. I wanted to be told I was beautiful and go to parties. I never got that.

Jean: No, no one is entitled to a charmed life. That's a fairy tale. You learn to work and negotiate for what you get.

Helen: That can't be true. I always tried to be what my parents wanted, instead of being myself. I hear thoughts echo in my head telling me, "I'm not good enough, try harder."

Jean: Now it's time to be yourself instead of what you think others want. When you try and be what others want, you deny yourself. You're treating yourself just like your parents did. Learn to talk back to your internal dialogue. Make it tell you what you want to hear, like "I'm okay just the way I am."

Helen: Okay. I'm bright and pretty.

Jean: How does that make you feel?

Helen: Good. I feel good with that.

Helen's control of her internal dialogue is an important aspect towards resolving her anger and resentment. Once she is able to provide that which she longs for, her anger will be easier to release.

INTERNAL DIALOGUE

Identify what your internal dialogue is doing to you, and change it to produce the feelings you want. Be very kind and supportive to yourself while the changes are being made. Once you notice a shift, continue the process, or you might relapse into old thinking patterns.

Your internal dialogue is like a record you made very early in life. The grooves are deep because you play it often. It is an ingrained habit that takes support and time to erase.

If your internal dialogue says, "I'm no good," then change it to say, "I'm just right the way I am." Watch out for put-downs, and be nice to yourself.

Some of your internal dialogue may contain irrational beliefs, such as *should* or *must* statements. "The house *should* be clean," is an example. When you *should* on yourself, you make life miserable. It may be nice to have a clean house, but why make it a burden? Ask yourself, "What would happen if it wasn't clean? Would the health department condemn it? Would my children be taken into protective custody?"

SHOULD AND MUST STATEMENTS

Should and *must* statements express expectations that create limitation about the way life is or isn't. You are controlling and manipulative when you make *should* statements to someone else. *Shoulds violate basic human rights.*

The more expectations you have, the more helpless you feel. Helen expected her parents to give her a charmed life. She wanted to be popular and go to parties in high school. When she wasn't invited, she blamed her parents. Thirty years later, she's still angry.

When life doesn't meet your expectations, you may feel out of control and even trigger a panic attack. Search out all your *shoulds* and kill them.

Shoulds are inherited from society, the culture and your family of origin. These perfectionistic *shoulds* are often rooted in fear of rejection. For example, will you be accepted and loved as you are? Resist giving in to your *must* or *should* internal dialogue.

It is important to write *should* statements down, and then find an antidote to each one.

When you don't follow through on your normal way of reacting to *shoulds*, you'll find your anxiety rising. It will peak and fade away. Each time you resist it becomes easier, until finally, no negative energy is left.

REPROGRAMMING OLD DIALOGUE

You do not live in a vacuum. When you catch yourself hearing old dialogue, say "cancel, cancel," to yourself. Then repeat a positive statement to replace the old.

Perform a physical act to reinforce your new attitude. Go to the mirror and say, "I accept and love myself as I am."

When you hear old dialogue, it's like watching an old movie on T.V. Simply visualize yourself changing the channel. The effect is stronger when you write down negative thoughts. After recording the negative, write down new positive thoughts. These changes are generative. Furthermore, you can keep upgrading your internal dialogue your entire life.

• On the most basic level, survival is the key issue. If your internal dialogue says, "If I don't please my mother, (friend, boss, anyone) she might desert me and I will die."

Say cancel, cancel to yourself, and state an affirmation, "I can take care of myself. I am not a helpless baby."

• The second level concerns power.

If your internal dialogue says "Others are perceived as stronger than I am. I must please them, or they may push me around or destroy me."

Say "cancel, cancel" to yourself and state an affirmation. "I have a power of my own. The more I use it, the stronger it grows."

• The third level deals with love and compassion. If your internal dialogue says, "If I don't please my husband, (wife, partner, lover) he may leave me."

Say "cancel cancel" to yourself and state an affirmation. "He can learn to accept me as I am. Only in being a whole person can I experience a true relationship based on love and respect."

• The fourth level is intellectual in nature.
If your internal dialogue says, "How do I measure up to what you want?"

Say "cancel, cancel" to yourself and state an affirmation to learn to set your own standards and live up to them, not someone else's.

• The fifth level is perception.
If your internal dialogue says, "It's okay to boss me around."

Say "cancel, cancel" to yourself and state an affirmation. "I believe and trust in my own feelings and intuitions. I can make my own decisions."

PERFECTIONISTIC TENDENCIES

Perfectionistic tendencies can cause you to feel overwhelmed. Doing the "right" thing according to someone else's standard is costly to your health and emotional well-being. Your authentic feelings may be muddled and confused when you feel driven by a compulsion to perform.

You may feel toward yourself as you thought your parents felt about you. Often, you carry the feelings of your parents unknowingly.

If feelings aren't discussed in the home as you grow up, you can unconsciously identify with the predominate feelings of your parents.

JANE

Jane, an attractive woman in her early thirties, began having panic attacks after her divorce. When she was young, her father rarely communicated with the family. A typical scene in her home was her father getting drunk and his head falling in the mashed potatoes as he passed out at the dinner table. Her mother, a rigid perfectionist, had heaped piles of *shoulds* on Jane. She felt fearful and inadequate.

During therapy, Jane discovered she unconsciously carried her father's feelings of inadequacy and her mother's untreated incest fears. It was a great relief for Jane to psychologically unload her parents and live her own life with her own feelings.

CONFUSED FEELINGS

Confused feelings are common if you don't feel or talk about them. When you don't acknowledge your feelings they won't get integrated. You can't learn from them or heal.

Dysfunctional families condition their members to all feel the same thing. Individual differences are discounted. If you say, "I don't like the color purple," a family member might counter, "yes, you do. We all like purple."

It's also common in dysfunctional families for parents to say one thing and do another. These behaviors produce confusion in children.

Serious and disabling problems arise from denial of your perceptions and feelings. You learn to not trust your feelings because you make so many mistakes in judgement. Your judgement is distorted, particularly in regard to relationships. When you can't trust your feelings, you seek affirmation from others to tell you what's real and what's not.

Mary Jo's father molested her when she was nine years old. She told her mother, who insisted it never happened. She forbid Mary Jo to talk about it. Twenty years later Mary Jo became paralyzed with fear. Deep hypnosis helped her to uncover her sexual abuse. Then she understood why she never trusted her feelings. She was taught not to.

JOURNAL

There are several excellent ways to help clarify your feelings. One method is to keep a journal. Journal writing helps separate out and integrate emotions. Here are some journal writing tips.

1. Keep it fairly neat and orderly.
2. Write at a specific time every day.
3. Stay focused for a minimum of twenty minutes.
4. Focus on the day's events: Feelings, thoughts, interaction with individuals and new awareness' in response to daily life.
5. Look at what's happened and how you felt and how you responded.
6. Periodically check back on previous days' writings.
7. Use journal writing as a sounding board for what you learn, experience, feel and see.
8. Look for patterns in your behavior.
9. Write everything down as fast as you can without judging it.
10. An alternate method involves asking yourself how you feel by writing with your right hand, and answer back to yourself using your left, or nondominant hand. This allows the child in you to speak directly from the unconscious, and unscramble confused feelings.

FOCUSING

Another method to decipher confused feelings is to relax, and silence the mind. Focus and concentrate on the confused feelings. Ask yourself quietly, "What is this trying to tell me?" Stay in the stillness and wait. An image or another feeling may appear, or you might hear something.

Don't analyze or judge your impressions, but accept whatever comes. Be aware of any feelings shifts in the body. Ask yourself, "Is this okay to be with?" If it is too painful, your body will tell you. If it is, ask yourself, "Is it okay to be with the inability to deal with the feelings." Then sense whatever the body presents to you. Befriend it. Embrace it as you would a hurt child. See the feeling not as an enemy, but as a friend and a teacher.

Notice how your body feels now. Compare it to when you started. You can stop when you wish. This method will usually leave you feeling better.

It may take several days to integrate whatever is brought up. If you do this several times a week, you will notice a dramatic shift to feeling better.

The body has a consciousness and wisdom of its own. This kind of knowing and sensing from the cellular level helps you get in touch with your feelings.

FEELINGS ARE PERCEPTIONS

Feelings are your perceptions of events, situations and people. They are neither right or wrong. They simply are. Once you experience a feeling, learn what that feeling has to teach you. Write it down and talk it through. Then release the feeling. Your body is not designed to hold feelings, and causes problems when you do.

GETTING IN TOUCH WITH YOUR FEELINGS

FEELINGS ARE ENERGY

Feelings are energy. When feelings aren't released, you feel tense. Stuck feelings can become lodged in various parts of the body. Anger can locate in the liver; fear in the long striated muscles, and anxiety in the heart. They then create blockages that may cause pain and disease. Whether you're aware of it or not, when you are angry and fearful, your neck muscles tighten. They can become so hard that all the blood circulation to the head is reduced. The pressure builds up. When your neck muscles relax, the blood shoots into the head. The engorged blood vessels put pressure on the brain which causes headaches.

Sarah came for therapy because she couldn't relax and didn't know why. During hypnosis, very painful feelings emerged about her husband. A year earlier, she had called him at work and asked him to take her to the hospital. He was too busy. She took a taxi to the hospital where she was operated on for a ruptured appendix. Within moments of feeling this emotional pain, a cyst in her breast, where she had held the pain, dissolved. Six months later she filed for divorce.

RELEASING FEELINGS

A meditation to release feeling is, "I surround ________ (person, event, situation) in love and light. I release them to their deepest and highest need." Repeat this as often as necessary. A lightness in your heart area will occur as the feelings evaporate.

Thank yourself each time you go through these exercises. The thanks establishes a link with your unconscious. The nicer you treat your unconscious, the more cooperative it becomes. Each time you get in touch with your feelings it gets easier to do so.

CHAPTER 5

IRRATIONAL THOUGHTS & BELIEFS

You use your senses of feeling, hearing, seeing, taste, and smell. But you have one sense you prefer. This dominant sense you use to make decisions, based on how it makes you feel, the way it looks to you, or whether it sounds logical. These senses, and many more subtle senses help you decipher your life experiences. Your language patterns then decode the senses to reflect your thoughts and beliefs.

These thoughts and beliefs are like wearing glasses with different tinted lenses. They can screen out most of the light, making life look dim and limited in choices, or they can let in the light. With light, life looks bright and full of promise and opportunity. Depending on the lenses you use, life will validate your perceptions.

If you think the world is a dangerous place, then what you think about, read about, and pick up on, will affirm your beliefs. If you think the world is a safe place, then your experiences will affirm that also, because that's what will get your attention.

SENSORY SYSTEMS

If you delete a sensory system, your outlook on life may become distorted, resulting in faulty decisions. Sensory systems are sometimes deleted when traumatic events occur which you repress, or because of mixed messages you received growing up. That's how conflicts are dealt with when you're vulnerable.

Each sense is located in a particular portion of the brain. To access a sense, look with your eyes in a certain direction:

- Up to the left is visual memory
- Up to the right is visual imagination and creativity
- To either side, left or right, is auditory (hearing)
- To the left is hearing memory
- To the right is where you will find constructed words
- Down to the left is auditory, also, but here you simply rehearse the pitch, tempo, and tonality of what you are going to say next.
- Down to the right is kinesthetic, (feelings), past, present, and future.

This pattern fits ninety-five per cent of the population. To discover if you have deleted any of your sensory systems, look up to the left, to the right, directly to each side, left and right, and down, left and right. If any of these positions feels strained or you simply can't put your eyes in the desired direction, that's a sign you're blocked in that sensory system.

To correct the condition, force your eyes in the blocked direction. This may feel uncomfortable at first, but the more you do it, the easier it becomes. This simple exercise can help restore your blocked sensory systems. The reasons you blocked them in the first place may present themselves.

Faded and repressed memories may reappear. Scenes of your parent telling you to do one thing and then doing another often surface. If you are programmed about the way life *should* be, you may delete your imaginative sensory system. You aren't able to imagine other possibilities. This results in an inability to have creative thoughts or ideas.

Learn to unblock yourself and create a life of your own choosing. If your eyes rarely go down to the right, into feelings, your emotions are inhibited. Frequently this results in intellectualized experiences. Other problems occur too, because you aren't in touch with your feelings and won't know when you're tired. You may keep working and working. Soon your body is under so much stress the muscles may go into a suspended state of contraction. Then all sorts of things can go wrong.

You might get migraine headaches, get sick, or have a panic attack. That's the body's way of communicating the need for relaxation. Doctors call it battlefield fatigue. You work until you get sick or have a headache. Then you rest. As soon as you feel better you get up and do it all over again. Professional people are extremely susceptible to this syndrome. Take time out. Give yourself plenty rest, and learn to pace yourself. Break this poor habit.

Record an interaction with a tape recorder, and replay it later. Notice your visual, auditory and kinesthetic or feeling terms. If you use only visual terms, such as "look at that," or "paint me a picture," you may be deleting other systems. Learn to use terms from all the sensory systems. You'll find your life becoming richer and more rewarding. Better yet, you'll have corrected a great deficiency.

As you unblock your sensory systems, thank yourself for having the courage and patience to integrate these experiences. Then release the emotional feelings connected with them. You may find that some of your beliefs are based on deleted sensory systems and repressed experiences. Ask yourself, "what has this experience taught me?" If an event that happened when you were five influenced your beliefs, you may wish to reevaluate it with your mature judgment.

BELIEFS

Some of your beliefs are helpful. Other beliefs are destructive, irrational, limit your choices in life and can actually cause a panic attack.

Beliefs are learned from your experiences, your family, and the culture. Catastrophic misinterpretations or beliefs can predispose you to develop panic attacks. Beliefs such as feeling numbness is a sign of a stroke; feeling dizzy means you might pass out; feeling breathless indicates you're suffocating, or feeling tight in the chest signals a heart attack. These beliefs are misinterpretations of physical sensations. The correct information about what is and is not harmful to your body is important to your recovery from panic attacks.

IRRATIONAL THOUGHTS AND BELIEFS

Our beliefs are like highways in the mind. Some of our roads are full of chuck holes and detours, while others are smooth six lane highways, filled with unlimited opportunities. What makes the difference? People learn to limit their choices in life. One of the ways is through rules. Some rules are designed to control you. They can be recognized by a *should* or *must* in the sentence. Very often a rule sounds like a command. "*Always* be nice." "You *must* be good."

Control type rules interfere with your spontaneity and make you feel as if you're living by a formula. Think of the resentment that builds up when you're always trying to please others! The "nice lady" role takes a heavy toll on some women. I once heard a famous doctor comment, "Breast cancer patients are so nice. If they'd only talk back and cause some trouble, break a rule or get angry. Then they'd have a better chance."

Rigid rules can take the fun out of life. Family rules dictate how members function. The *no talk* rule stops members from talking with "outsiders" about the problems they experience in the family. Rigid rules stop you from getting the help you need.

If you are programmed to be good and not cause trouble, often you'll feel guilty and seek punishment when you do cause someone trouble. What if you don't feel like being *good*? What if you go to a counselor and discuss family problems. Then you'll find your anxiety rising because you're in conflict with your family's *no talk* rule. For a few days, notice your behavior, internal dialogue, and your reactions. Look for rules. Once you have identified one, ask yourself if the rule is to your advantage, or not. If it's not helping you, mentally visualize dumping the rule into the garbage.

The brain loves novel and creative ways of learning, and unlearning. Make up your own ways of releasing less than useful beliefs and thoughts.

In the process of decoding the world, human beings learn to generalize. This provides for rapid learning. Once you learn how to open a door using a door handle, you can generalize and open most doors. However, if you're bitten by a dog, and generalize that all dogs bite, then this can cause pain and limitation for you. Generalizing from one experience can lead to phobias. If you get rejected by someone you care for, you might be afraid to start a new relationship. The thought, "What if I get rejected again?" may haunt you. The fears of rejection, abandonment, and engulfment are all generalized from primary experiences.

When you use generalizations, you delete the individual characteristics of people or situations from your awareness. "All men are brutes," deletes the possibility of recognizing a man who is kind, warm, and gentle. Whatever image you have of a man or woman exudes a certain energy on the unconscious level.

Unconscious energy operates on strength and frequency, so you attract the same type of energy you put out. When one woman said, "All men are brutes," I knew that was her internal image, so that's what she attracts. She'll continue attracting that type until she changes her internal image of men. Interestingly, her internal masculine image is actually a part of herself that she projects onto that sort of man. If you wish to read more about projecting parts of yourself onto other people, *Jung to Live By*, by Eugene Pascal deals with this subject in depth.

Distortion is the process of making the world fit your beliefs. Self-fulfilling prophecies arise from distortions. If you don't think you're lovable, you're apt to put up walls and miss opportunities for new friendships. Distortion occurs when you remember only certain aspects of a memory, and not all the details.

If you believe you had a good childhood, you may have only pleasant memories. Negative events, such as abuse, get repressed, and then you wonder what's causing the panic attacks.

Distortions occur in other ways too. When you think someone is feeling this or that way, and you don't check it out, you're doing a mind reading trick. A paranoid person may imagine something, believe it's true and act on it. The difference between a paranoid personality, and one who uses mind reading, is that the paranoid type is always sure of being right.

"What was your childhood like?" I frequently ask clients. Often the answer is, "Normal, I guess. I don't remember much." That answer reflects inner turmoil. It takes lots of energy to repress memories. The more you repress, the more pain you hold in the unconscious.

The more you repress, the more forgetful you are about everyday things. The unconscious isn't selective. It can take many things into repression, leaving you with blanket memory loss. You have good days and bad days. On your good days, your defenses work better. On bad days, memories or tensions may break free and surface. Sometimes you can't remember anything at all. You feel unbalanced. Your brain may feel mushy and sluggish, as if you simply can't think.

When you make up a reason for the way you feel, you're using "emotional reasoning." One man, who had been away on a long business trip, found that as he drove closer and closer to his home, he began feeling tense. As the tension increased, he panicked. He imagined his wife having an affair, and decided that caused his tension.

When he got home, he accused his wife, yelled and screamed at her, and threatened to beat her up. By this time, there was nothing she could do that would convince him she wasn't having an affair.

Only later, during counseling, did he understand he manufactured reasons for his feelings. This type of emotional reasoning can be dangerous.

EXPECTATIONS

Expectations limit your choices in life. They are beliefs about the way the world is and is not. The more extensive your expectations, the more dependence and lack of direction and control you have over your life. Some expectations are goal oriented and realistic. For example, when you sit down to a Thanksgiving dinner, the turkey *should* be cooked and tender. The dressing *should* be done. These *should's* cause pressure. What if it isn't done? Will the world end? Expectations lead you into pitfalls and create unnecessary discomfort.

Learn to identify an expectation. It is usually stated with a *should* or *must* in the sentence. "You *should* be happy." What if you aren't? Does that make something wrong with you?

Expectations are created by things happening over and over the same way until it becomes a fact of life. "We *always* eat Sunday dinner with my Mother." Does that sound familiar?

Break expectations by asking yourself, "What would happen if I didn't? Would the roof fall in on my head? Would Mother be mortally wounded and never speak to me again?"

The more expectations you have, the greater the tendency to be attached to authority (parental) figures, and the more you try to please them. Children feel an instinctive need to protect their parents. Obviously, they can't take care of you if they're not safe and well. Not protecting them may produce certain fears: loss of love, rejection, or fear of punishment. In fact, a certain amount of guilt can be evoked if you break one of the family traditions.

Always is another word that denotes expectations. "This is the way things are *always* done at my house." Couples who have recently married usually find that, after the honeymoon is over, they begin to fight about the differences they bring from their families of origin. "In my family we *always* keep Christmas this way."

If you actually want to do something different, ask yourself, "*Always*? Has there ever been a time when it was different? How do other families handle it?" Chances are you'll find enough exceptions to break the family rule and do something else if you wish.

Expectations may cause you to feel hopeless, trapped, and isolated because they create limitations and block out opportunities. They work against you, not for you. To find out if you have an expectation, analyze where it comes from. Does it belong to another person, society, or is it just a habit? Expectations are passed down from parent to child, generation after generation.

Expectations hurt relationships when you insist loved ones behave in certain ways. You can become sad and disappointed when they don't.

Sue's boyfriend took a long trip. Before he left she extracted an agreement from him to call her once a week. When he didn't, she became agitated, and panicked. She felt he was abusing her by not calling. When he did call, she berated him for lying and told him how much she suffered. His telephone calls became even less frequent, and Sue began to fear he might end the relationship.

When you impose expectations on others, they may be experienced as manipulative and controlling . Even when you intend the best for your loved ones, allow them the gift of their own free choice. Expectations create problems by programming you to feel differently than you actually do. Depression sets in when you judge your feelings and worry that you're not feeling the *right way.* If you think, "I *should* be happy. After all, I have a nice home, a good husband, job, children, and yet I'm not happy." You worry, "What's wrong? I did everything right. I should be happy." This type of thinking—the repetition of thoughts—fires off the neurons repeatedly. Mental fatigue develops. A greater distance is then created between the actual state and the desired state you wish to achieve.

Your irrational thoughts and beliefs can be identified by making a chart of all your *shoulds, musts, always,* expectations, deletions and distortions. Correct them by asking yourself, "Why *must* I," and, "according to whom?"

CHAPTER 6

FANTASY & IMAGINATION

Jana spoke to her Toastmaster's group: "Have you ever had a spell or attack when you suddenly felt frightened, anxious, or very uneasy in situations when most people wouldn't be afraid?" Jana's hands and legs shook as she clutched the podium to steady herself.

Toastmasters had helped Jana overcome her fears of people ridiculing and criticizing her. However, now, her blood pressure increased as she talked. Her neck and chest broke out in red blotches. Before therapy, Jana practically apologized for breathing. Now, she could talk to a group of people.

With dogged determination, Jana continued her speech. She looked at the audience smiling at her, giving her encouragement. Suddenly, the image of her mother standing over her, pointing her finger at her, and ridiculing her, flashed in her mind so vividly she wondered if she had hallucinated it.

Jana took a deep, slow, breath, and continued her talk. A new sense of pride emerged within her. She realized it wasn't the world, or strangers, or friends she feared criticizing her. It was her mother's ridicule that frightened her. She wasn't crazy. She had been reacting to her mother's harpy condemnation.

Her hands and feet stopped shaking. She knew her Toastmaster's group had her best interests at heart. Her voice sounded stronger than ever as she finished her speech and heard the rounds of applause.

Just like Jana, your vivid imagination, fantasies and feelings may not make sense to you, but you're not crazy. You simply don't know how to interpret unconscious reactions. For example, in the unconscious, there is no time frame—everything is now.

Helplessness once felt in childhood such as the abandonment, and rejection, are active fears until each is resolved. These anxieties and fears seep into consciousness through your dreams, imagination, fantasies and behavioral reactions. But, they are distorted.

Instead of your mother, it may feel as if strangers are out to criticize you, or you're wearing a "hit me" sign on your back. Until, like Jana, you piece the puzzle together. Then it makes sense.

FANTASY AND IMAGINATION

Because panic attack victims have been conditioned to block out logical thoughts and deny their feelings, they frequently don't distinguish fantasy or imagination from reality. The result is magical and catastrophic thinking. As long as thinking isn't followed by action it's called fantasy. Imagination is nothing more than entertaining an idea.

You may think what comes from your imagination and fantasy is reality and create irrational reasons for what you feel. "If I feel tense, that means something's wrong," or "*what if* . . . ." You then imagine the worst that could possibly happen and see terrible outcomes to a situation.

WHAT IFS

What ifs are culprits which can summon up enough fear to stop you from doing almost anything. For most panic attack victims, the intervals between panic attacks are consumed with worry about when another attack might strike, and what else can go wrong. And, of course, the pump is primed for the next attack by thinking about having one.

What if I have a panic attack?

What if I don't make an A?

What if I'm not perfect?

What if I __________?

So what! Will the world end? Will you be shot at daybreak? This type of imaginary thinking is known as catastrophizing. Remember the fairy tale of Chicken Little? She walked around with a leaf on her shouting, "The sky is falling, the sky is falling." Chicken Little's reaction is a classic example of catastrophizing.

Sam had some problems on his job, and "was written" up on one occasion. Then a new boss arrived. Sam felt threatened by him, even though he had met him only briefly. He began to catastrophize. In his imagination, Sam saw himself receiving a pink slip, clearing off his desk, and walking away from his job forever. He thought about it constantly.

His anxiety skyrocketed. Soon, he developed panic attacks. He became forgetful and made serious errors at work. His fears perpetuated a self-fulfilling prophecy. He orchestrated every step of his firing.

Sam developed a pattern of rejection. He had five jobs in quick succession. Finally, discouraged, he refused any more interviews. He felt cursed, and continued to vividly imagine what next disaster might befall him. More losses followed. His wife left and his home was repossessed. In Sam's mind, he responded to whatever he felt or imagined as reality, so his fears came true.

Many things in life are like a two-sided coin. It is important to remember that talents and abilities can be used for positive or negative ends. Sam might have used his exceptional abilities of imagination and visualization to propel him to the top of the success ladder, not the bottom.

BLACK BORDERS

If you have internal visual images and think that's reality, you aren't separating fact from fiction. One way to overcome this is to imagine a fantasy in your mind. Then image it as a framed painting. Put *black borders* on all four sides of the painting.

Create several fantasies in your imagination and put *black borders* around them. Your images concerning reality won't have borders.

Close your eyes for several minutes and do this. Once the unconscious gets the idea of separating reality from fantasy, it will do it from then on.

Imagination and fantasy are the language of the right hemisphere of the brain. Usually everyone has one side of their brain that is larger and dominant over the other. This dominant side determines overall preferences and personality characteristics.

RIGHT AND LEFT BRAIN HEMISPHERES

Dr. A.L. Wigan, a physician in Scotland in 1844, performed an autopsy on a friend who had led a normal life. It revealed the deceased possessed only the left hemisphere of his brain. This started the "two mind investigations" that surmised the left hemisphere is the smart side. The right one was thought to be a spare tire! Since then, numerous studies have investigated the functions of the right and left hemispheres.

Panic attack victims rarely use their left hemisphere for logical thought analysis to complement their vivid right hemisphere imagination. Instead, hunches or guesses are used for decision making instead of logical thinking through things.

The right hemisphere is often called the feminine side. It functions primarily as the connector to the inner worlds of feelings, creativity, imagination and symbols involving the unseen and unknown.

If you are uncomfortable with things you can't see, feel or touch, you're not tapping the full potential of your right brain. You may not trust what comes to you from the right brain, or place much value on it. If you manufacture internal images of disaster, it's your right hemisphere processing the possibilities from "the world is a dangerous place" programming. Fear then emotes from lack of knowledge and experience.

The left hemisphere of the brain is often referred to as the masculine side. It controls functions in physical reality:

- how to go to the grocery store
- how to fix the toaster
- how to balance the bank account

Left brain dominant people are often thought to be inflexibly systematic. Their life motto is, "Show me a rule and I'll follow it to the ends of the earth."

INTELLECTUAL CURIOSITY MISSING

Intellectual curiosity is often missing in panic attack victims. Perhaps this is due to their lack of confidence in controlling their lives. If you're stressed, you probably prefer the movies to Shakespeare or an illustrated magazine to difficult reading. Whenever reality becomes unpleasant, daydreams and fantasies become substitutes for intellectual reasoning. You focus on passivity and receive emotional gratification at the same time.

You may have fantasies of "Prince Charming coming to take you away and everything will be all right." Or, you might envision romantic interludes during which you experience sexual arousal, including sexual fighting scenes. The feelings disappear when you are confronted by reality. Fantasized emotions may be used to avoid real feelings, especially rage.

Laura felt numb around people, but when she was alone, Laura had rapturous feelings and vivid fantasies of going places and doing things; having lovers and reaching the heights of sexual excitement.

But her feelings disappeared whenever her husband wanted sex. Her hands trembled. During her therapy, Laura discovered her childhood incest, and processed the fears and rage about it. Then her hands stopped shaking, and she could access her real feelings all the time, including being sexual with her husband.

HIGHLY SUGGESTIBLE

Panic attack victims are often:

- deficient in the knowledge of "how to do"
- highly suggestible
- easily influenced by another's opinion
- easily influenced by the pressure of real or imagined expectations
- may take a suggestion as a command

BRAIN BALANCING

Not using both halves of your brain is like driving a car with half of the cylinders missing. Ideally, both sides of the brain communicate with each other. When you have an image, the left, logical, masculine side thinks it though. If you want to learn something, the right, feminine side finds creative ways to learn it.

Some people work hard their entire life to achieve a goal, while others arrive at the same goal with a minimum of effort in a fraction of the time. The difference is using both hemispheres of your brain simultaneously. Brain balancing is one of the keys. Here are some exercises to balance both hemispheres of your brain using visualization.

EXERCISE ONE

The first exercise is to visualize yourself as a man, for the left hemisphere, and a woman, for the right hemisphere. Allow these two people to get to know each other in every way men and women relate. You might start by having them meet one another. Progress to a visualization where they go on a picnic, or perhaps share a spiritual experience. You might visualize the couple in love with each other and exploring their sexuality. Be wildly creative in designing visualizations for the man and woman in you. Let them communicate and really know each other.

Do these visualizations on a daily basis for five weeks. This exercise teaches the right and left brain hemispheres to cooperate and work together. You might also trigger "healing dreams" by doing these visualizations before you go to sleep.

EXERCISE TWO

Another method of balancing the left and right brain hemispheres, is to tilt your head to one side. Imagine one hemisphere filling with water. Slowly move your head to the other side, and imagine the water flowing to that side. Do this several times, until you can feel the energy moving from side to side. This exercise opens up both hemispheres to work harmoniously.

The stronger the energy you exert doing these exercises, the quicker you get results. If you make fear-based visual images and fantasies, simply recondition your energy to utilize the same processes for developing confidence and a better life for yourself. Visualize for success, not failure. As you check out your internal images with your logical side, make your creativity work for you, not against you.

The left, logical, side is intellectual and wants to know *how to do* things. It wants the one and only *right* answer. The right, feminine, side creates feelings and inspiration. It doesn't require a *right* answer, but offers many answers. To stimulate them to work together, be aware of the pull from both sides, but remain neutral. Stay open and develop the ability to tolerate ambiguity.

EXERCISE THREE

Plato's Phaedrus dialogues discuss the soul drawn in a chariot by two horses—one black and one white—pulling in opposite directions. This has been a powerful image throughout history.

Imagine you're the chariot driver. Controlling the horses to go where you want is equivalent to harmonizing the two halves of your brain to work together. This archetypal image can be very powerful in helping you adopt a course of action.

BREAK UP NEGATIVE IMAGES

Changing subtle parts of an internal image, such as sound, color or speed, helps release traumatic memories. You can shift the image to brighter or dimmer, the sounds louder or softer, or the speed slower or faster. When you recall times you felt helpless and victimized, you probably remember them in your mind the same way. By distorting the image in some way it loses its power.

- If you are afraid of criticism and fantasize people frowning at you, visualize them with long donkey ears, and enjoy a good chuckle.
- If a scene of your boss chewing you out keeps playing like a broken record, play it backwards. Change the color, or the sound, and speed it up so your boss talks in a high, squeaky voice.
- If someone has abused you, and you're still fearful, imagine your abuser in a cell behind iron bars.

- If you see a frightening image, imagine you have a ray gun and bombard the image with white light until it explodes.
- If you have had an unpleasant experience, and it keeps bothering you, play the scene over by visualizing it from different locations. Have the encounter take place in front of you, to each side, from up above, and looking up at you from under the floor. The feelings associated with the experience will probably diminish, if not vanish.

Make up your own changes for internal images to counteract the destructive patterns that keep you a prisoner of fear. Your creativity, when used for positive purposes, is unlimited.

JERI

Often, persistent fantasies develop from unresolved events left over from childhood struggles. They are often accompanied by feelings of pain, rage and helplessness. No one would guess that during the past eighteen months, Jeri had spent over one hundred thousand dollars trying to find out what was wrong with her. Jeri was an attractive thirty-two year old. Her long, dark, brown hair silhouetted her petite figure. Her hair had never been cut and hung to her hips.

Jeri was extremely enterprising, and owned a successful advertising agency that, among other things, developed slogans and songs for national companies. But a persistent fantasy permeated her thoughts. She feared being kidnapped, and went to great lengths to avoid being alone.

"It happened suddenly," she said. "I was drawing a cartoon for an ad. My body felt as if someone had thrown me to the ground. I've never been in such pain. I thought I might die. It frightened me, so I went to the hospital and took every test imaginable. But they found nothing. It wasn't physical. "Then everything went along as usual for a while. Another time I was in my apartment and the same thing happened. I fell to the floor. My entire body ached and throbbed. I couldn't move for hours. I just lay there in pain. When it was over, I went to the hospital and stayed for a week. Again, nothing. The attacks continued to happen over and over. I've been to the most noted doctors in the world. But no one seems able to help me. The doors to my mind seem locked."

Her history revealed that her parents divorced when she was two, and she never saw her father again. Her mother died shortly after the divorce, and an aunt reared her. Jeri had tried for years to locate her father. The following dialogue was excerpted from thirty biofeedback sessions, when Jeri was in a deep state of relaxation utilizing brain wave biofeedback equipment. She was emotionally detached from her body and feelings while she observed what happened to her.

"I'm standing at the top of the stairs. My mother has me wrapped in her arms. My father's pulling at me, trying to get me away from her. They're fighting. My mother's foot slips, and we fall down the stairs. She doesn't move. I think she's dead. My father grabs me from my mother's arms and runs away. Now we're in his car. I'm crying. I'm scared and frightened. We drive around all night. At daybreak, he drives back to the house and pushes me into some shrubbery around the house and drives off."

Jeri's pain was her body's memories returning. She had fallen down the stairs with her mother. But she had more to deal with than that. She had lost both her parents suddenly. Now the deep sadness of her losses surfaced, and she started a profound grief process. One that may take years to resolve. Childhood grieving is different from losses sustained in adulthood. The process takes much longer, and the grief is harder to heal.

Jeri's fear of being kidnapped was a clue to finding out what happened to her. If you have horror fantasies, or enjoy horror movies, this might be a clue about your forgotten past; a past containing abuse and abandonment. When you're wounded, you don't always know what's hurting you. You might create fantasies to explain the pain. Look deeper into your own psyche. That's where the answers lie.

CHAPTER 7

STRESS CATCHERS AND COPING SKILLS

Shortly after Mary Ann went to work as a nurse at a small hospital she learned many nurses had high blood pressure. When her own blood pressure elevated, Mary Ann analyzed the tension that caused it. The patients were challenging to work with. That wasn't the problem. When she asked some of the other nurses how they felt, a common remark was, "My efforts don't count. I feel suppressed by the higher ups."

The pecking order at the hospital was directed by a doctor whose primary concern was the enhancement of his own ego. Next in line, was his henchwoman, the head nurse, and then came the many underlings, including Mary Ann.

Mary Ann was shocked by the occasional cruel treatment of patients. She saw the head nurse threaten to hit an unmarried pregnant patient, force her to do vigorous exercises against her will, and call her a "no good little whore."

When Mary Ann expressed her ethical concerns about the protection and rights of patients, she was told, "That's the way things are around here. There's nothing you can do. If you want your job, keep quiet."

Mary Ann filed a complaint. "Why do you think we're so stressed? It's hard to live with something that's incompatible with our value systems, but we need our jobs," several nurses told her. "The Doctor is God, and we're all his little handmaidens. You filed a complaint against his chief handmaiden. They're out to get you. Better look for another job." And she did.

It's not always that easy to identify or resolve the source of stress in your job or relationships. Awareness is a key. Once you know what causes your stress, you can choose to see it differently.

You can choose how it effects you by altering your response to individuals, events, and situations. You will inevitably encounter difficulties and frustrations in life. But it's your *attitude* and reaction to a situation that stresses you, not the situation itself. Stress has its roots in your thoughts and shows itself in your body. What is stress for one person may be for another, all in a day's work.

Some things you have little control over—external stresses of noise, pollution, heat or cold, or rigidity in a job, for example. Physiological changes also cause stress—menopause in women, aging, illness, accidents, poor nutrition, and sleep disturbances.

Your reaction to environmental threats may also cause stress, or you may decide a certain situation is dangerous.

You can't avoid stress. And, it's not all harmful. Stress results from any change in your life, anything new you learn, or any behavioral adjustment you make. A new home, a new marriage or job all create stress. And yet, their challenges can be exhilarating.

Internal stress involves your perceptions. *Should* and *must* statements are stress catchers. So are holding on to feelings, taking things too personally, and thinking negative thoughts. If your boss gives you a frown, do you think he's angry with you, or just has something on his mind?

Stress may result when there's not enough time for all the things you need or want. Job pressures, financial difficulties, demands of parenthood, interpersonal problems or constant behavioral adjustments add up. Events from two years ago may continue to effect you. Problems can occur on the mental, emotional, physical and spiritual levels when you are too stressed.

When they do, your accumulated stress causes your muscles to tighten and knot up, and blood pressure to rise. That triggers the *flight or fight* response. A panic attack can occur. It's your body's way of letting you know it has had enough. If you are stressed, reflect on how you're reacting to pressures and take time for yourself and rest.

STRESS TEST

The following stress test will give you an idea how much stress you have. Score each item from 1 (almost always) to 5 (never), according to how much of the time each statement applies to you.

___ 1. I eat at least one balanced meal a day.
___ 2. I sleep six to eight hours a night.
___ 3. I drink less than three cups of coffee a day.
___ 4. I have a regular exercise routine (running, tennis).
___ 5. I have a network of friends with whom I share problems.
___ 6. I don't have more than four alcoholic drinks a week.
___ 7. I smoke less than half a pack per day.
___ 8. I have good health.
___ 9. I have enough money to meet my needs.
___ 10. I am assertive when necessary.
___ 11. I have friends or relatives who will help me if I need it.
___ 12. I have a spiritual belief.
___ 13. I have a regular social circle.
___ 14. I take time to relax and be by myself.
___ 15. I have good luck.
___ 16. I do something for fun each week.
___ 17. I am organized.
___ Total Score

To get your score, add up the figures and subtract 17. Any number over 28 indicates a vulnerability to stress. You are very vulnerable if your score is between 48 and 72, and extremely vulnerable if it is over 73.

STRESS TOLERANCE

Stress tolerance refers to how much stress you can tolerate and still be effective without it hurting you. Knowing your body's stress tolerance level is important to maintaining an even balance. Just the right amount of stress and tension is useful and can serve as a motivational factor. It's also important to recognize your body's warning signs prior to going into stress overload, so you can slow down.

If you don't you might get headaches, nauseated or your eyes might twitch. When stress continues to accumulate, you can become depressed, anxious, and unable to cope.

STRESS BUILDUP

There are three phases of stress buildup. In the first phase, the body signals an alarm and triggers the *flight or fight* response. The brain releases hormones and chemicals to help fight the stress. When this happens, your heart begins to race and you may perspire.

The second phase is called the *resistance.* Adrenaline and other hormones are increased to either resist or adapt to the stress. This phase prepares you to deal with crisis. By definition, a crisis has a beginning, middle and end, with an approximate duration of three months. If the conflict remains unresolved, muscle tension develops and the muscles may go into a suspended state of contraction. Obvious ailments are tension headaches, spastic colitis and chronic back problems, to name only a few. The treatment for muscle stress is relaxation and exercise.

In phase three, prolonged stress exhausts and depletes the body. Prolonged stress has negative effects on the body, mind and soul. The hormones and chemicals your brain releases to help you fight stress cease to be effective. Neurotransmitters become ineffective. Your digestion, immune system and the inflammatory responses shut down. Alcohol or drugs may be abused trying to relax.

Chronic stress and tension contribute to major depression and panic attacks. You can't concentrate or make decisions under chronic stress. Your sexual drive decreases, and you may feel irritated, frustrated and have angry explosions. An uneasy feeling of being lost in life and not knowing where you're going may permeate your thoughts. Headaches, muscle tension, fatigue, arthritis and disease may develop. These are the results of too much stress and failure to adapt.

WARNING SIGNS

Stress warning signs include:

- feeling unable to slow down
- explosive anger in response to minor irritations
- tensions that last more than a few days
- inability to focus attention
- boredom
- sexual problems
- sleep disturbances
- cold hands and feet
- indigestion
- heart palpitations
- constipation
- low-grade infections
- overeating or under-eating
- increased intake of drugs or alcohol

BODY AWARENESS

Body awareness is a key tool for fighting stress. Where you hold stress in your body is unique to you. Neck? Shoulders? Solar plexus?

To find out, sit comfortably in a chair, close your eyes and take a few deep breaths and relax. Begin to notice where you feel tension and where you don't. Take your hands and feel over your body. Search out tender or painful places. That's another clue to locate where you collect stress.

Around the heart area, and in the soft spots on the front of your body under your shoulders, are two classic places people hold tension. If these are tender, rub them until the pain is gone.

Other remedies include placing your palm over the tender area. Ask for your body's healing energies to come to that spot. Feel the energy from your hand radiate into the area. Visualize pink light flowing in and loosening up the tightness.

Other common tension spots are the lower back, which frequently symbolizes you don't feel very supported by life. Upper back tension may symbolize you feel you're carrying a heavy burden.

Dialogue with the different parts of your body. Put your finger on the part of your body that feels tense and then put some pressure on it. Relax and close your eyes. Ask your body what the tension is trying to tell you. Listen for the answer in the stillness. Perhaps you will receive an image, or a thought may emerge.

Look in the mirror and notice if one of your shoulders is lower than the other. If it is, close your eyes and imagine you are holding a bag in the hand below the lowered shoulder. Exaggerate it and feel the heaviness of the weight pulling you down. Then put the bag down, open it and see what comes out.

Neck tension and tight muscles can cause headaches. The back of the neck is one of the places where repressed anger collects. Holding feelings and not expressing them is a primary cause for building up stress, pressure and tension. When neck muscles tighten and knot up, the blood flow can't get through the muscles to the brain. Blood pressure builds up behind the stricture. When the muscles relax, the blood shoots into the brain, engorging the blood vessels. Blood spills out of the vessels, puts pressure on the brain and causes a headache.

If you notice your neck muscles tight, massage and loosen them. Ask yourself, "What's causing me to hold tension here?" "Am I angry about anything?" Wait and listen in stillness for the answer.

ANGER

Anger is an emotion that almost always results in stress unless you're good at letting it go. Realize your own reason why releasing anger is a problem. Perhaps you're not comfortable expressing anger. Do you live in a financially dependent relationship where expressing anger will jeopardize your security? Grow up in a family where anger wasn't acceptable? Work in an atmosphere where you feel suppressed and can't be yourself? Some people are shamed and conditioned to think they have no rights at all. They don't know anger is an option.

Obviously, anger can be very complex. Some people get mad when they don't get their way. Some allow themselves to be taken advantage of. Some have repressed anger from childhood abuse. Some may feel the need to be perfect and are frustrated. And some don't feel at all. They're not aware of having anger, only headaches.

It helps to identify the source of your anger. Once you do, find a way to release it or resolve the conflict. Writing out your feelings of anger can be especially helpful. Hitting a punching bag or pillow, or screaming out your frustration usually brings some release, even though it probably won't solve the problem.

Assertiveness may be one solution. Compromise may be another. Ultimately, the source of your anger needs to be dealt with. If you're extremely uncomfortable with anger, consult a counselor to help you learn how to express it.

STRESS JOURNAL

To discover more about your stress level and its symptoms, monitor them by keeping a dated journal. When you feel tense or have a symptom, analyze what is going on right then, and the twenty-four hours preceding it.

For example, if you have a headache, you would put down, headache—fight with spouse. Or, sick to stomach—the kitchen plumbing broke and the repair bill came to $400.00. Or, dizzy and feel like I'm losing my balance—felt threatened by a co-worker. If you have a menstrual period, note when you have it and if that contributes to your stress. Also record if you have had more than three cups of coffee.

Learn to trace the cause and effect of your internal world of thoughts and feelings and your external world of happenings. Identify how you react to them and the symptoms they produce. Ask yourself what happened an hour ago and write that down. Then go back to two hours ago, a day ago, and so on. Reflect upon them.

Now, approach it another way. Ask yourself when was the last time you had symptoms and what was going on in your life then. Continue to trace it back to the time before that, and the time before that. Continue to trace the symptoms to the very first time they occurred. Notice the emerging patterns. After several days of tracking your reactions and symptoms, you'll discover the why, what and how of them.

AUTOMATIC RESPONSES

If your stress reaction is an automatic response, decide how you want to respond differently. Practice visualizing the new behavior in your mind until it feels like second nature. When you start to react in old familiar stressful ways, tap into your new resource behavior.

If there is proportionately too much stress in any one part of your body, you probably need diversion. Take a break from your routine and go to the movie or take a small trip. If there is too much stress in the body as a whole, you must rest.

ATTITUDE AND STRESS

You can control your stress on many different levels. Your attitude is one level. A lot of stress comes from seeing, hearing, and feelings things you either don't want, or fear, in your life. Having a positive attitude, allows stress to go through you, like wind blowing through the trees.

To turn the spiral of negative stress into a positive force, ask yourself, "What stops me from realizing this is an opportunity to overcome my negative attitude?"

Think positively, and position yourself with flexibility, versatility, and control. Different outlooks on life allow stuck habits and ruts to fade away.

If something happens in your life and you say, "I don't like this," or "I don't want this," (both are stress catchers) change it to "How can I make what happened useful for my purposes?" Leave it open, and don't try to solve it immediately. Let your creativity work for you. Perhaps, a week or month later, the answers will return to you.

When you make a habit of taking whatever comes to you and utilize it for positive purposes, you can take the sting out of negativity and stress.

When you detect stress, notice the muscles tense up. The hardness of the muscles, like an imaginary suit of armor, tries to protect you from threat.

Tense muscles trap energy in them. Jump up and down and shake your arms and legs to break up the frozen pattern. Physical activity is a great stress reducer. When you do it prior to having a quiet time of reflection, it makes relaxation and meditation even more effective.

RUNNING THE LIGHT

A relaxing and energy clearing technique, which also untangles balled up energy is known as *Running the Light.* It is a variation of the technique described in Chapter 6. Find a location where you won't be interrupted. Begin by sitting in a chair with your hands on your knees. Close your eyes and relax as much as possible.

Imagine the white flame of a candle above your head. As you breathe in, imagine the white light from the flame coming in the top of your head. Focus it in the space between your eyebrows. As you breathe out, imagine the white light flowing through your brain, down your neck and shoulders to your hands. Hold the white energy in your hands.

Return your attention to the top of your head. Breathe in the white light again, and run it down your face, neck, torso, and hips. Pick up the light in your hands and run all that down your legs and out the soles of your feet. This two-part exercise is extremely helpful. Continue doing it as long as you feel comfortable. Any tension, images or dark spots you might internally see, simply run them out the soles of your feet. Some people see a muddy river running out of their feet, with the images of things they've held onto for years.

A powerful form of this exercise is to feel your pulse beats, then, when you breathe in, breathe in for six heart beats. Hold your breath for three heart beats while you focus the white light between your eyebrows. Breathe out for six beats as you run the light down the body and out of your feet. Hold your breath for three more beats while you return your attention to the top of your head. This continuous cleansing breath and visualization of breathe in six beats, hold three, breathe out six, hold three, is very strong and powerful.

MELISSA

To help her relax, Melissa did this exercise in a tub of hot water. Once, after doing it for several hours, she reported seeing and feeling a black oily glob moving out of her head, down through her body and out her feet. When she saw the image of her father, she realized she had a great deal of pain associated with their relationship.

During her adolescence, they had had many fights and arguments. She left home bitter. Melissa hadn't seen or talked to him for years. During her meditation, she realized she was, "Just as stubborn as my father."

Shortly afterwards, Melissa took a vacation from work to visit her father in another state. She told him how much she loved him. They both wept, and renewed their relationship on a much better level. He felt good about it, and so did she. The problems Melissa had been having in her relationships with men disappeared when she resolved her problems with her father.

Because Melissa relaxed deeply, it allowed her to think about her relationship with her father in a new light. A lot of stress comes from stuck feelings, as Melissa had, and seeing, hearing, and feeling things you either don't want or fear.

You can reverse the spiral of negative stress, and turn it into a positive force, by asking yourself, "What stops me from realizing that the stress I am experiencing is actually an opportunity to reach a new level of awareness. I can choose to see this differently." When you maintain an open mind, stress can flow through you instead of getting stuck in you.

WORDS THAT CAUSE STRESS

You can create tension by the words you use. If you refer to someone as "a pain in the neck," long enough, you will probably end up with just that. Calling yourself names, such as "I'm stupid," or "I look awful" also provokes stress.

"Thought stoppers" is a good remedy for this affliction. Whenever you detect yourself engaging in negative criticism, say **STOP**. Some people wear a rubber band around their wrist and snap it whenever they start to degrade themselves. It's an excellent way to break the negative habit.

STRESS COPING SKILLS

Overstress is a sign you lack coping skills. Relaxation is a coping skill. Relaxation induces a number of physical changes that counteract stress. These include a lowering of the heartbeat, a lessening of muscle tension, and lowered levels of blood pressure and cholesterol in the blood. Exercise is a coping skill. You can practically jog away your stress. Taking a walk in nature or beside a body of water will also ease your tensions.

Self-talk is still another coping skill. For example, if you think, "I'm panicking, I've got to go home," these thoughts increase your fears and your symptoms may escalate until you leave. Instead, let your thoughts tell you:

- It's O.K.
- I can do this.
- Stay calm.
- Relax.
- Remember to breathe.

Stress coping thoughts tell your body there's no need for arousal. In the middle of any stressful situation, you can say a series of fear conquering statements.

- I've survived this and worse before.
- There's an end to it.
- Keep focused in the present.
- Relax.

You can dialogue with yourself and give encouragement while you encounter stressful situations. In preparation for a stressful situation, talk to yourself, say:

- There's nothing to worry about.
- I'm going to be all right.
- It's easier once I get started.
- Keep calm.

As you confront the negative situation, tell yourself to stay organized, take it step by step, and not rush. Say to yourself:

- I can do this.
- I'm doing it now.

- It's O.K. to make mistakes.
- Easy does it.

Remind yourself frequently to relax, breathe deeply, and that there is an end to it. After you have experienced the stressful situation, reward yourself by doing something special. Tell yourself:

- I did it.
- Next time will be even better.
- It's possible not to be scared.

It's best to make up your own stress coping statements because they will be personalized for you. Write them down and take them with you wherever you go. Refer to them if you start to panic.

Place them in handy places where you can see them often, such as on the refrigerator door and bathroom mirror. Cut out pictures from magazines of people doing the things that you desire to do, and place them beside your stress coping statements. Let the pictures remind you, *if it's possible for someone else, it's also possible for me.*

Laughter is a stress breaker. Prepare a laughter "first-aid" kit. When you feel stressed out, take a break and go to a funny movie, look at cartoons, or read a short, humorous article. It helps to stop taking things so seriously.

Another antidote to painful stress is to paint your emotions with water colors. You don't need a fancy easel or art lessons. All you need is your imagination. Allow it to flow onto the paper. Some people like to use oils, and use their fingers to smear the color on. Still others like to mold their emotions in clay. These mediums allow you to express yourself creatively.

Art therapy works wonders. Long recognized as the conductor between mystical inner worlds and outer realities, art therapy can reach levels words cannot describe.

Prayer is a stress reducer. By offering your thoughts and concerns to God, you learn to let go and let God handle it. Your prayers may be answered in many ways. It may not always be in the way you want it, but it will be in a way you can learn from it.

Organization helps to manage stress. Make a list of things to do. List them in order of importance—and make an ending! If you can't draw a line on a day's work, you are in the perfectionist trap; trying to do everything. Another way organization can help is to list everything you can think of, and do just one or two things a day. You may find some of the things you thought were important really weren't, and you can eliminate them. Making a lists helps to give you perspective on what needs to be done. It also clears things out of your brain and you don't have to keep trying to remember everything.

Write down the things that stress you and what you can do. Then read them aloud. Take action if possible. If not, put the list away for a day and forget it. When you get the list out the next day, are you still stressed?

Wait a week and see if the stress resolves during that time. If you can't resolve it, can you learn to adapt to it? Can you get a new perspective on it?

When you feel overstressed with limited choices, relax and take a mini-vacation by mentally projecting yourself onto a deserted beach. Imagine you find a brightly colored talking parrot along your path.

When you feel very relaxed and peaceful, ask the parrot, given your situation, what he would do. This technique opens up your creativity to work for you. You may get solutions you would never think of, helping you to resolve the stress.

The synergism of brainstorming with friends also generates numerous solutions and plans of action.

So does dreaming. Analyzing your dreams can give you stress reducing answers for your life. Ask your Higher Self for guidance in your dreams.

Every problem has many different solutions. How many can you find for your situation? Some of them may involve change. You may need to be more assertive, develop coping skills or build up confidence by practicing thought control or visualizations.

Utilize goal setting along with problem solving. Set a time limit to achieve each goal. Rank order them, from the most important to the least. Goal setting helps you to stay on tract, and not wander off into a swamp of self-pity and despair.

Some cultures have tiny worry dolls. Each doll is given a worry and placed in a basket. The doll is assigned the responsibility of worrying so the owner doesn't need to. Later, the dolls are taken out and asked if the worry is solved.

Regardless of how you tackle stress, there are many realities to recognize and accept.

- You can't have everything.
- Things won't always go your way.
- There is injustice in life.
- Some people will never understand you.
- You can't please everyone.
- Traffic is slow during rush hours.

CHAPTER 8

SPECIFIC PHOBIAS

Marie laughed nervously as her eyes darted to my degrees on the wall. "I feel silly being here. I'm really normal. But I've become terrified of dogs. Six weeks ago, I left my six year old daughter, April, outside to play while I visited with a neighbor. By the time I heard April's cries and ran outside, a growling and biting dog had her on the ground. I grabbed the dog by its hair and pulled it off April.

"We rushed to the hospital's emergency room. April was treated for head wounds. "Why did the dog bite me? I only wanted to play with him," April asked me. "She loves animals. Later, we discovered the dog had been hit by a car, and hadn't "acted right" since. So the dog was put to sleep."

"Whenever I see a dog now, I get fearful, light-headed, and sweat. So, I avoid them. It doesn't interfere in my life, but now I dream of a dog attacking me. I stab and kill him with a knife."

Soon after Marie started therapy, her father suffered a heart attack and died. "It's strange," Marie spoke softly. "As soon as I left the funeral home, I saw a large, gray, dog. It took me several seconds to realize I wasn't afraid of the dog. Then a relief came over me, and my fears vanished. My body felt radiant."

"What does that mean to you?" I asked.

"I adored and idolized my father," Marie said. "I remember wanting to say some parting words to him in the coffin, but I choked. I felt frightened of him. We never had conflicts because I always pleased him. It occurred to me, I might have more than one way I felt toward him." She looked at me curiously. "I was scared of him, and never knew it. Could that be?"

"Yes, it's highly possible you denied your fears and covered them up by idolizing your father. You didn't see him as a real person with strengths and weaknesses. But there's more. Because you feared your father, you were probably also angry with him. By repressing those feelings, you avoided struggling with your ambivalence."

"Yes, that feels right. But why? I never had a phobia before. Where were my feelings?" Marie yearned to unravel the mystery that grew deeper with each question.

"You probably repressed your fear until the dog incident. You're no more aware of repressing something than you are of forgetting something. The same fears you had repressed were triggered when you saw the dog attacking your daughter. You displaced those feelings about your father onto the dog. I wonder what your father did that made you so fearful?"

Marie stared off for a while, then shook her head. "I don't know. He was a good man."

After asking her mother some very pointed questions, Marie learned her father drank heavily when she was young. He had sexually abused her repeatedly.

Marie's mother had filed for separate maintenance and insisted he stop drinking. Her father had joined AA and the family reunited. Marie's parents had agreed not to talk about the abuse, thinking she'd forget it. But, a part of her remembered, and when she saw the dog attack her child, it triggered her early fears. Marie displaced her unconscious fear of her father onto the dog, and then avoided dogs.

Marie is not alone in her fears. According to The National Institute of Mental Health, women have more fears and phobias than men. Women report consistently higher numbers of fears and higher intensity levels of those fears. Complex but surprisingly common, phobias may affect between twenty-four to forty million people of the United States. Phobias are the second most common lifetime mental disorder, second only to alcoholism.

Phobias take many forms. They are very common and a few people are incapacitated by them. Some people can't ride elevators, some tremble and hide at the crack of thunder and some never leave their homes.

While the association between fear, anxiety, panic and phobia is very close, there are important differences. Everyone experiences anxiety from time to time—your first day on a new job, for example. This is a healthy type of anxiety.

Free floating anxiety indicates you're having doubts or

insecurities about your life. You constantly survey the environment wondering, "What can go wrong?"

At the bottom of most insecurities is, "Am I going to get my needs met? Who's going to take care of me?" Don't underestimate the strong dependency needs left over from childhood.

Anxiety also comes from irrational thoughts and feelings about failing, being trapped, embarrassed or ridiculed. This unhealthy anxiety comes from defective belief systems, such as, *the world is a dangerous place.*

As panic attacks increase in frequency, a new type of anxiety develops, called *anticipatory anxiety.* You anticipate something frightening—hours, days or weeks—in advance of an event. You start thinking, *what if's.* "*What if* I get panicky when I go to town?" "*What if* I feel trapped and can't leave?" Anticipatory anxieties are situation oriented head trips and set you up for more panic attacks.

Fears arise from lack of experience, knowledge, confidence, the unknown, and traumatic events. They can be intense enough to cause physical symptoms. Emotional reasoning and imagined catastrophic consequences can trigger fear reactions. Fears usually involve a real, imagined or symbolic threat to survival. "I feel bad. That means something's wrong with me." "*What if* the elevator gets stuck?" "*What if* the snake gets out of the cage at the zoo?"

If you become overwhelmed by fear and anxiety and coping mechanisms fail, a panic attack may strike. When panic attacks increase or become more intense, you may develop phobias to displace the fear and anxiety onto the situations and objects where panic attacks occurred.

The phobic situation or object is then avoided, and the fear and anxiety are contained in the phobia. You may think your fears are silly, childish, or trivial and try to conceal them. While hiding from your fears, you might hide your phobias from others, which limit your experience of life. It's better to tell someone.

There are three types of phobias

- specific phobia
- social phobia
- agoraphobia

The most common is specific phobia, the unreasonable fear of some object or situation. Specific phobias, especially animal phobias that arise from actual childhood encounters, are very common in children. They are usually outgrown. If they persist into adulthood, treatment will probably be required.

The fears can start in childhood or adulthood. Some people suddenly become terrified of things they've done for years. For example, a man who owned an airplane and flew regularly, became afraid to fly it.

Adults can usually sidestep their specific phobias, concealing their fear and distress without much difficulty. If the phobic object is rare or easily avoided, such as a city dweller being afraid of snakes, it's not going to cause much trouble.

Even those who usually adjust their lives to fit their phobias are sometimes able to confront their fears, "toughing it out," suffering all the while. Though children may outgrow their phobias, adult's phobias usually don't remit without treatment.

Animal phobias nearly always start in childhood. Blood-injury phobias usually begin in adolescence or early adulthood. Phobias of heights, driving, closed spaces, and air travel occur most frequently in the forties. Mid-life crisis stressors—anxiety of being trapped in life's circumstances, the emerging shadow side of the personality, and the desire for independence—triggers the forties' phobias. Obviously, you can't leave (spouse, job, town) if you're afraid to fly or drive the car.

A tendency to be high-strung or nervous, coupled with a poor ability to cope with stress, increases your vulnerability to phobias.

A specific phobia frequently begins during an acute panic attack or traumatizing event. The anxiety and fear that erupts during the ordeal are displaced to an external object or the place where it occurred. Phobias also start by having an overwhelmingly fearful and shocking experience. Note the following example:

Two boys are playing. One of them sees a snake, picks it up and throws it at the other boy. When he sees it flying at him, he becomes terrified and panics. Afterwards, he becomes frightened every time he sees a snake. He can't even go into the snake house at the zoo because it triggers his fear reaction. Twenty years later, he's still afraid of snakes.

CHARACTERISTICS OF PHOBIAS

The outstanding characteristic of a phobia is a persistent, excessive fear of an object or situation that is not dangerous. The phobia begins when you actually start avoiding the object or situation. When you are in a phobic situation, you may experience physiological reactions such as excessive perspiration, tremor, racing, pounding heart beats, rapid breathing, diarrhea, vomiting, and tightness in the chest.

You might realize your fears are irrational, or rationalize them. This doesn't make you any less anxious or fearful. Most phobics make statements such as, "I'm afraid but I don't know why." "I feel like I'm going crazy." "I feel as if I'm about to explode or burst," or "I'm losing control."

What you become phobic about usually depends on where you are when a panic attack strikes. If you're driving a car when you have a panic attack, you may avoid driving your car. If you're in a grocery store when you have a panic attack, you may avoid the grocery store. You associate the fear experienced during the panic attack with the object or place where it happens.

The anxiety that erupts during panic attacks, and becomes attached to things by association, may occur several times before a phobia is established. You go to the grocery store on different occasions and have several panic attacks there before you start avoiding the grocery store.

However, if the panic attack is severe enough, it might cause a phobia the first time. That makes life more tolerable because you can avoid the situation or object. Your fear and anxiety are then contained by the phobia. You don't feel anxious except in the phobic situation.

Avoidance only feeds the problem and makes it worse. Rewarding yourself by fleeing feared situations and objects conditions you to find relief by avoidance.

Phobias develop because it's very rewarding to avoid frightening situations and feel relief. So that action is repeated over and over.

COMMON PHOBIAS

Some of the most common specific phobias are:

- heights
- dirt
- the dark
- open spaces
- odors
- storms
- strangers
- flying
- germs
- closed spaces
- dentists
- illness
- being in a swimming pool
- falling

Phobias can spread if the original phobia isn't strong enough to contain the fear and anxiety. Then, every time you have another panic attack, a new phobia might spring up. Another way phobias spread is to generalize.

A person who is phobic about knives, for example, may generalize that not only knives, but all sharp objects are dangerous, and then include scissors and ice picks in the phobia.

Some phobias may be extremely disabling. Eventually, you may have so many things or places to avoid you can't leave your home.

There are many different kinds of phobias. Any object or situation may be the focus of one. Like dreams, phobias may have some universal symbolism, but remain basically subjective. Only the phobic knows their true meaning.

Few people seek treatment for their phobias. Either the phobia doesn't interfere in their life enough, and/or they are embarrassed about their fears. Or perhaps they don't understand what's happening to them, and consider themselves weak for allowing something like this to interfere with their life.

Those who do seek treatment frequently go from doctor to doctor seeking cures for the physical symptoms that accompany their phobias.

Often, even the doctor fails to recognize that stomach pains, high blood pressure, rapid heart beat, and other symptoms may indicate intense fear. Unless questioned, patients may not think to mention their fears. Doctors may not ask. While the bills keep mounting, the condition fails to improve.

It takes eight to ten years for many phobic persons to find appropriate treatment. During that time, they may see ten different professionals.

New treatments for phobias are remarkably effective. Much of the pain and disruption—perhaps most of it—can be remedied.

Few people, including doctors, know about the treatment techniques for phobias.

You don't have to know or understand the underlying cause of a phobia to recover. But you must confront the object or situation you avoid. Techniques to overcome phobias are included in Chapter 11.

CHAPTER 9

SOCIAL PHOBIAS

Social phobias are distinguished from specific phobias by the nature of the fear. Situations are avoided, not because of fear of having a panic attack as in a specific phobia, but because you're scared of doing something or acting in a way that will be humiliating or embarrassing. Panic attacks can occur, but the panic is related more to being embarrassed or humiliated than to feeling trapped.

If you are a social phobic, you're intensely afraid of being judged by others. Even at a social situation, you expect to be singled out, investigated, and found wanting. You may even feel "on trial" in social situations. So you avoid them.

Because of these fears, you are scared to let others see your vulnerabilities, and scrutinize peoples reactions to you. The essence of social phobias is you'll look like a fool in front of someone else.

You might be afraid to go to a party because you fear other people will laugh at your clothing or think you're stupid because you can't think of anything to say.

You fear humiliation or embarrassment if you show anxiety in front of others. Ironically, you're often so inhibited that you have difficulty thinking or talking clearly. Even success in social situations may fail to make you feel more confident. You might think, "Next time I'll fall on my face."

Social phobias frequently start in late childhood or early adolescence; about the time peer pressure becomes important. Social phobias usually result from childhood conditioning. You may have had a parent who was exceedingly critical of you, phobic, timid, or shy, or you may have never developed social skills. Phobics frequently report being shy and isolated as children and adolescents.

Unlike specific phobias, which almost always require treatment for adults, social phobias can be overcome with experience and maturity. You can recover from social phobias by gradually exposing yourself to situations you prefer to avoid. Taking a class in assertiveness training, joining Toastmasters (an international speaking club designed to assist people overcome their public speaking fears) and working on self-esteem issues will help you gain confidence. You can be comfortable in social and performance situations. *But you must confront your fears.*

CARLA

When Carla came for counseling, she was twenty-four years old, depressed, not working, and sleeping on her parent's sofa. She called herself "socially retarded." She felt awkward making "small talk" in social gatherings and avoided places where she might need to interact with others. Growing up, she had received little guidance from her parents. As she described it, "I only wanted a tidbit of attention from my parents, but none came."

Carla was given homework assignments as a part of her therapy. First, she went to a department store and bought something. When she could do that easily, she went to the next challenge.

Shy and lacking friends, she took a painting class at an art museum, and showed me several pieces of her art work that were quite good. To Carla's surprise, she was invited to join an advanced group. She struggled with the offer because she felt "out of her class." It wasn't in her self-concept to feel wanted, even though she was extremely bright and talented and possessed a pleasing personality.

Carla eventually joined the group and became an accomplished artist. She developed other talents and volunteered at a community service organization as well.

As she progressed in her therapy, she expressed fear and concern about her sexual feelings. At one point, Carla attributed sexual significance to almost everything and everyone with whom she came in contact. She laughed during one of her sessions, "If I really let myself go and lost control, I'd rip my clothes off and run naked through the streets and sexually attack every man I saw!"

Once she accepted her sexuality, Carla discovered she could be comfortable anywhere she went. In accepting new dimensions of herself, Carla made some close friendships. But most of all, she exchanged her social phobias for confidence. She eventually worked her way through college, got a job, moved out of her parent's home and bought a home of her own.

SOCIAL PHOBICS ARE OFTEN AFRAID OF:

- blushing
- humiliation
- crowds
- job interviews
- embarrassment
- using public toilets
- signing their name while others watch
- eating or drinking in public
- standing in line
- public speaking
- social situations
- parties

The most common social phobia is fear of public speaking. It effects performers, speakers and students who have to speak before class.

In some theaters, brown paper bags are kept offstage for the actors to breathe into to offset the effects of their hyperventilation from stage fright.

Although social phobias are usually not incapacitating, marked anticipatory anxiety occurs when you confront the phobic situation—sweating, feeling panicky, rapid heart beat and difficulty breathing.

Considerable inconvenience may result from avoiding the phobic situation. Trips may have to be postponed, dates canceled, and fear of public speaking may hinder a promising career.

Until you stop avoiding, and start confronting your social phobias, they can restrict and affect your entire life-style, your relationships, and influence your choice of jobs.

One woman changed her major in college from education to history so she wouldn't have to practice teach. She became fearful anticipating standing in front of a class speaking. When her employer relocated, another woman changed jobs so she wouldn't have to take the elevator.

While many people suffer from social phobias, few seek treatment, even though social phobias are relatively easy to cure using therapeutic methods.

TRAITS AND CHARACTERISTICS OF PHOBICS

These traits and characteristics are often present in the phobic personality:

- low self-esteem
- feelings of worthlessness
- constant worrying
- perfectionism
- the fear of anger or conflicts
- self-criticism
- dependency

Without treatment, phobics usually remain immature due to emotional conflicts revolving around dependency issues. They are extremely suggestible, naive, and unreflective; uncritically accepting procedures that border on the magical. One therapist issued his client a *safety pass*, which he carried to assure him of safe passage when he went somewhere.

Men are reported to have social phobias more frequently than women, and often use alcohol and drugs to conceal their distress. Episodic abuse of alcohol and drugs is common in social phobics.

Studies estimate that between five to ten per cent of phobic people become dependent on some chemical (such as alcohol) as a means of self-medication to cover up their anxiety and cope with their symptoms.

Harry is a recovering alcoholic who works on my ranch. When I told him I was writing a book on panic attacks, he related his own experience with phobias. "It was years ago, when I had so many fears," he said. "I was afraid of tall buildings because I thought they would fall on me. Sounds crazy, but it's true. I was reared in the country, and growing up, I hadn't been around tall buildings. I'd drink whenever I had to go to the city. "One night, I got as drunk as I could and still stand up. Then, I drove to the city and went down the street with the tallest buildings. I got out of my truck, looked up at them and shook my fist and cursed at the tall buildings for making me afraid. I stayed there till daylight. Then, I threw my bottle down and never drank again. I guess that got me over it."

SAFE PERSON

Others may not use alcohol to help them confront phobic situations, but have companions to accompany them wherever they go, to prevent them from experiencing acute panic or anxiety. Such companions, often a husband, wife, or child, may become very dedicated. The companion may be used as a symbolic parent—a *good mother,* or *safe person* who protects them from their fears. Always present in phobics, is an unconscious wish to be taken care of. They want their dependency needs satisfied. But overprotection, love, and support won't help master situations. You need to learn this for yourself.

CHILDHOOD FEARS

If you have a phobic personality, you probably had multiple childhood fears: fear of the dark, of snakes, swimming, animals, or fear of being hurt. You may regress, and reactivate these fears when difficult hurdles must be faced in later life. Or, you may copy a phobic, timid, parent who communicates those attitudes to you.

Much of your behavior is learned from your parents. One expert estimates as much as ninety per cent of behavior is learned by observing parent's actions: how to communicate, how to solve problems; how to face the world. You may not be aware of it, but you model the actions of adults you observed while growing up.

Phobias may cover up other problems. School phobia, a complex condition in which a student refuses to attend school, is usually diagnosed as separation anxiety from parents. The child may actually be having panic attacks due to other psychological problems.

Patty, a young teenager, refused to attend school. Her mother was very concerned and brought her for counseling.

"May I see you privately before the session," her mother asked. Once inside my office, her mother handed me a tattered notebook.

"It's Patty's diary. You should see what's she's writing about."

"No" I said firmly. "That belongs to Patty." I walked into the reception room and motioned for her daughter. When we were all inside my office, I handed the notebook to Patty. "This belongs to you. I haven't read it."

"Oh, that's just great. I can't have any privacy at all," Patty grimaced.

"What do you mean?" I asked.

Sheepishly, Patty looked at her mother, and then back at me. "I mean," she said clearing her throat, "Mother goes through all my things; my drawers, my notebooks, everything. I don't have anything I can call my own."

"Of course you do," her mother said defensively. "I have to protect you."

"That's not protecting Patty. That's smothering her. Stay out of her things and allow her some privacy," I said sternly.

Patty looked astonished that I would talk to her mother that way. The next day Patty returned to school. Within a month, she had been elected cheerleader, and had many outside activities with her school friends.

By developing her school phobia, Patty protected her mother from the emptiness in the mother's life. Patty didn't want her mother to feel the pain and loneliness of her barren existence. So Patty narrowed her world by refusing to attend school. Then her mother didn't have to confront what she was missing in her own life. Patty's world was in front of her, her mother's life was gone, except for Patty.

Even though the "real problem" belonged to Patty's mother, Patty had taken it on by developing the phobia. When Patty gave up the school phobia, she stopped protecting her mother and started living her own life.

Many phobias are more complex than they seem. And their "irrational" nature may be an attempt to solve a real life problem, or a failure to develop social skills. After a period of time, the phobia takes on a life of its own, regardless of its initial unconscious purpose.

In order to recover, you need to resume the maturational process—learning to trust your feelings, having confidence in your abilities, thinking for yourself—and to release the blocks that prevented you from attaining independence.

Specific techniques to confront your phobias are included in Chapter 11.

CHAPTER 10

AGORAPHOBIA

An agoraphobic client was afraid he'd die if he left his home. His therapist bet him $1,000.00 he wouldn't. The client left his home for the first time in over six months, and, to his surprise, he lived. Even though therapists don't often bet money with their clients, agoraphobia, distinguished from the specific and social phobias by the large number of acquired phobias, frequently results in being house bound or immobilized by the multiplicity of phobias.

In fact, many people who suffer from panic attacks and phobias may go on to develop agoraphobia. Often, agoraphobics don't leave their homes unless accompanied by a friend or relative—a *safe person*.

The National Institute of Mental Health reports that between 2.7 and 5.8 per cent of the United States adult population suffers from agoraphobia. Women are affected two to four times more often than men.

EARLY CHILDHOOD LOSS

Agoraphobics frequently report the death or loss of a parent or other shocking event during their childhood. Feelings of abandonment and repressed unresolved grief haunts them. They assume the distressing events happened because they were "bad." They then try to make up for it by being "good" and pleasing others so they won't be abandoned again. This emotional blocking and patterning forms a destructive lifetime habit, leaving them unable to meet their own needs.

Many agoraphobics develop symptoms in their early twenties, shortly after suffering another loss, such as a serious illness or the death of a loved one. The loss triggers the unresolved grief from childhood, making them feel overwhelmed and shattered.

NEED FOR PROTECTION

The remaining parent is often described as timid, perfectionistic, overcritical, and overprotective. That parent may have transmitted attitudes that *the world is a dangerous place*, thus hindering the maturation process. The illusionary need for protection spawns strong dependency needs. Even after agoraphobics grow up, they might feel like little children.

If you're agoraphobic, you probably have average or above average intelligence. But, perhaps you were overprotected and overcontrolled; devoid of the necessary experiences that teach you how to maneuver in the world. Safety may become equated with being taken care of, a common wish in a phobic person.

INHERITED VULNERABILITY

Research suggests that agoraphobia often runs in families. This implies a genetic (biological) component. This research is used to support a theory of inherited vulnerability towards developing agoraphobia. Just as some people have brown hair, and others blonde, some people have more sensitive delicate systems. As one herbalist put it, "Some people are like BMW's and some are like Mack trucks. The Mack trucks can eat whatever they want and get by with it. And abuse doesn't put a dent in them. The high strung BMW's require more care and maintenance."

If you're hypersensitive, watch what you eat, exercise regularly, process your thoughts and feelings, and think positively. Because awareness is usually heightened in agoraphobia, you look for danger signs and perceive and imagine consequences faster.

If you catastrophize, you can easily get overwhelmed. One woman, shopping at a garden center, was solicited by a gardener for a job. After she gave him her name and address, the shop owner, who had overheard their conversation warned her, "I don't know that gardener, so I can't recommend him. Be careful, because sometimes gardeners steal things from your garage." Before she left the shop, she imagined the gardener raping and killing her.

"If I'm not heard from again," she said as she left, "his name was Bennie."

This extremely sensitive woman exhibited lack of logical thinking, catastrophized thinking, and imagined the ultimate loss, her own death.

BELIEFS

Beliefs play an important role in determining what makes you anxious or fearful. Most agoraphobics have anxiety sensitivity (numerous beliefs that anxiety is harmful that intensifies the fear reaction). Your fears are stronger and you experience them more often. The more anxiety-promoting beliefs you have, the more vulnerable you are to agoraphobia.

A common anxiety promoting belief is that anxiety is dangerous—a rapid heart rate signals an impending heart attack—but a person who has few anxiety beliefs regards a pounding, racing heart as uncomfortable. The more you fear your symptoms, the more you might avoid anxiety-provoking situations.

Beliefs about anxiety's harmfulness can be acquired in numerous ways: modeling of behavior by parents, spoken communication, including misinformation, as well as through panic attacks.

AGORAPHOBICS FEAR

The National Institute of Mental Health reports agoraphobics most commonly fear the following situations:

- Tunnels or bridges

- Being in a crowd
- Being on any kind of public transportation like airplanes, buses, or elevators
- Going out of the house alone
- Being alone

When a panic attack strikes, you may feel so threatened, and have so little emotional reserve, all you can do is retreat. Once the retreat starts, it's hard to stop. You avoid places where panic attacks occur for fear of stirring up more emotions and symptoms.

PUT THINGS IN PERSPECTIVE

It's important to examine events a year prior to the first panic attack. These events are usually ignored. As you put the first panic attack in perspective with what else was happening in your life, you'll understand it really didn't strike, *out of the blue.* You were probably under a lot of stress and pressure at that time.

Agoraphobics frequently think of themselves as weak and inadequate, like young children in need of protection. Emotionally, that may be partly true.

Emotional reasoning, based on your feelings rather than on logical deductions, leaves you guessing for answers to questions instead of finding out for certain. This imaginative thinking may turn into catastrophizing; creating more feelings of helplessness and vulnerability.

Agoraphobics often judge their day by whether or not they had a panic attack or how uncomfortable their symptoms were. If you have a good day, it means you didn't have much anxiety. "This won't last long," you might say to discount it.

HOW AGORAPHOBIA BEGINS

If you have agoraphobia, chances are it developed something like this: One day, while taking a walk or driving to work, a wave of panic suddenly struck. Your heart pounded, you had difficulty catching your breath, and you trembled. You were convinced something terrible was happening. Maybe you were having a heart attack, or were going crazy. You went to the doctor. But the doctor found nothing wrong, so you went on your way. Then another panic attack struck, and you spent more and more time thinking about them. You worried and waited with fear for the next attack to hit.

You avoided situations where you had experienced an attack, then other situations where you would find it difficult to escape and get help. You started making minor adjustments in your habits—going to a supermarket at midnight, for example, rather than on the way home from work when the store is crowded. Gradually, you got to the point where you couldn't leave the house without a *safe person*, or couldn't leave at all.

Agoraphobics may not have panic attacks, but simply restrict their lives. You may attempt to control other people and your environment so that you're never surprised and your feelings aren't triggered. The major fear of the agoraphobic is loss of control. Strong feelings make you feel out of control.

Some experts think a conflicted marital relationship, in which the woman feels trapped and cannot leave due to separation anxiety, economic reasons, and a need to retain her passive feminine role, can cause agoraphobia. You don't feel independent enough to make it on your own, and the constant turmoil of a poor relationship debilitates you.

If you have agoraphobia, you are sensitized to what other people think about you, what you look like and what you wear.

If you're in a store, you might feel obligated to buy something. You expect others to judge or belittle you, making you feel powerless and inadequate. Often, these fears seep up from the unconscious and get displaced on to strangers.

Fear of embarrassment haunts you. You try to please others and have difficulty standing up for yourself and your rights. Like other phobics, you worry that someone might recognize your anxiety and make a hostile comment about it.

SAFE PERSON

Often, a companion or *safe person* accompanies you wherever you go to prevent you from experiencing anxiety. Because you monitor your feelings, fears arise about what might actually happen if you are alone and your tight control slips.

Agoraphobics have an irrational fear their body may not perform properly. If the companion leaves you alone, you get anxious. The companion, frequently a child or husband, derives satisfaction and pleasure from being needed. The companion may symbolize a parent—a *good mother* who protects you from your fears, or keeps you from acting on your impulses. *You can't lose control if there is someone present to manage you.*

But in other instances, your fears and helplessness may be used to break up relationships you resent to insure exclusive possession of your companion. Obviously, he can't be with someone else if he's with you.

MISINTERPRETATION OF PHYSICAL SENSATIONS

Agoraphobics frequently interpret minor physical sensations as the beginning of some catastrophic threat to life. For example, you may think heart palpitations indicate an impending heart attack, or breathlessness as a sign that you're suffocating, or racing thoughts mean you're losing control or going crazy.

Ironically, fears generated from such thoughts trigger the *flight or fight* response, panic attacks, and the strain eventually leads to actual physical problems—peptic ulcer, high blood pressure, skin rashes, tics, tooth grinding, hemorrhoids, headaches, and muscle aches.

Cardiovascular disease may develop. Doctors frequently do not relate these symptoms to fear, panic attacks and agoraphobia.

ALCOHOL AND DRUG ABUSE

In an attempt to control your anticipatory anxiety, you may abuse prescription drugs and alcohol to avoid feeling a loss of control.

Studies at several alcohol treatment centers indicate one third of the alcoholics admitted for treatment also had agoraphobia or a social phobia.

Using alcohol to self-medicate and diminish your sense of fear can become more disabling than your original symptoms. If you do become chemically dependent, you must first address that issue by attending some type of recovery program.

DEPRESSION

Depression affects most agoraphobics because of their restrictions, limitations and social isolation, as well as unresolved emotional losses and conflicts. Melancholy moods may plague you throughout life. Agoraphobia, with depression, is a much more serious condition than without depression, and it usually takes longer to recover. If you don't feel good, it's hard to get motivated to tackle anything new. The longer you're depressed, the more your thinking gets distorted and the less energy you have. Grieving your losses helps you recover faster.

PAULA

Paula, a pretty, twenty-five year old woman with hollow looking green eyes and dark circles under them, came for counseling following her divorce.

"I can't sleep. I'm so depressed. I'm afraid to go out unless someone's with me. I really think that's why my husband divorced me. He tired of my constant whining about my fear. Now, he's found someone else," she sobbed. "Look at my wrists," she held them out for examination. "I've tried slashing them three times." Tiny white scars marred her wrists.

"Thanks for telling me that. I want you to contract with me that you won't make any more attempts," I requested.

"That's a relief," Paula sighed quietly, "to find someone who'll listen to me. It's awful being confined to my house like a prisoner. I don't like begging people to accompany me. Doing things on my own, that's what I want."

"I'm glad you're motivated. That helps," I said. "Why don't you tell me some things about your early life. That often sheds light on how you acquired your fears."

Paula described her childhood and what it was like growing up in her home during the following sessions. Her early childhood showed a similar pattern to others I have seen with agoraphobia. She suffered a loss early in her life, which was never dealt with. Her father went to the military when she was four years old. While he was gone, her grandfather, whom she had shifted her attachment to, died. Her father returned home three years later, an alcoholic/addict. Frequent arguing and violence became part of her home life.

Her parent's marriage had deteriorated, and they rarely spoke to each other. Even after her father had gone to a treatment center and stopped drinking and using, there was friction between them. Her mother had moved into Paula's bedroom by the time she was an adolescent. Her mother then focused most of her attention on Paula, making her a surrogate spouse.

Paula's mother had tried to run her life for her. Afraid of her father's violence, Paula felt she had little choice but align with her mother. Her mother had picked out her clothes, friends, and her husband. She even made the arrangements for Paula's wedding.

"Mother," Paula had said, "I'm not ready to marry. I've got to get out of this."

"Nonsense, the presents have already arrived. I'm not going to be embarrassed by sending them back. You're getting married," her mother had replied.

"So I married him. That's what mother wanted me to do," Paula said shaking her head.

"After our marriage, Bob traveled. I was terrified at night. At first, I stayed up all night with a shotgun, and slept in the mornings. Then, I tried drinking until I passed out. That way I could get a little sleep before the alcohol wore off. Finally, I went to a doctor. After I described my symptoms, he said, "You're the anxious type. Once it starts, you'll probably be that way all your life. Get used to it." And then he gave me some sleeping pills."

Paula felt worthless and depressed. Her first panic attack had struck while shopping at the mall. She then avoided places where she thought she might have another panic attack. She became increasingly dependent upon her friends to accompany her.

Paula felt unprepared to take care of herself in the world. While she was growing up, Paula had learned to agree with others to avoid arguments or conflicts.

She had denied her own needs, hoping others would protect and take care of her. By the time she came for counseling, she was numb. She didn't know who she was or how she felt. She had repressed her anger.

But when it did surface, she flew into a rage. She didn't have a self to control it. She threw and broke things and tore up her clothes. As Paula put it, "I really wanted to kill myself. When I couldn't do that, I destroyed everything else I could get my hands on."

She had uncontrolled moments of terror, and shook all over with fear. She was always preparing for the worst, always on guard. Her life revolved around shoring up her feelings, and the next imagined disaster.

Paula had a tough job ahead of her—grieving her childhood losses, recovering lost memories, and learning new coping skills. She had to learn how to think for herself, how to be on her own, and how to take care of herself.

All her life her mother had said, "Find a man to take care of you." That hadn't worked, nor would it. Paula had to change the very fabric of her being.

At the same time that Paula needed a complete mental and emotional overhaul, her depression overwhelmed her. She struggled with guilt: guilt over being divorced, guilt over not taking care of herself, and guilt if she did take care of herself. She was trained to be subservient and please others. While she denied her needs and feelings, an even deeper fear surfaced of not taking her place in and with the world.

Paula needed more than agoraphobia treatment. She needed in-depth psychotherapy to change lifelong patterns.

TREATMENT FOR AGORAPHOBIA

Not everyone needs intensive psychotherapy, but professional help is usually needed to overcome agoraphobia. The ideal treatment for agoraphobia consists of ten to twelve weekly group sessions involving education about the disorder provided to both agoraphobics and their families. Treatment consists of:

- cognitive restructuring
- training in diaphragmatic breathing
- visualizations of encountering feared situations
- prolonged exposure homework assignments (actually confronting the phobic situation)

Treatment not only reduces anxiety and avoidance, but also the fear of anxiety. It's important to realize help is available on any number of levels. You can go to a treatment center for agoraphobics, you can choose to see a counselor and/or join a self-help group, and you can use the techniques described in this book. You can improve regardless of the severity of your problem. Eighty to ninety per cent of agoraphobics conquer their fears with treatment. Set tiny goals for yourself at first, ones you're sure you can attain. Then slowly work up to harder challenges. Success breeds success. Specific techniques to overcome agoraphobia are included in Chapter 11.

CHAPTER 11

PHOBIA REMOVAL TECHNIQUES

If you've ever been afraid of going to the dentist, you're not alone. Twenty-five to forty million people have dental phobias—so afraid they avoid the dentist for years. Today, most trips to the dentist are relatively painless. It's the anticipatory anxiety that triggers your fears. Here are some tips to help you make your next visit more tolerable. Eat a light meal before your visit. Don't drink caffeine but protein, such as a lean beef sandwich, can help stabilize your blood sugar and reduce your jitters.

Think positively, and repeat phrases such as "I can do it." "It won't be much longer." "I can stop if I feel uncomfortable." Remember to breathe deeply. Slow, paced breathing allows you to relax better. Take breaks during your treatment, and get up and walk around occasionally. Listening with headphones will distract you and muffle the sound of the drill. Use your imagination to think about things you like, or create a scene, for example, of walking on a deserted beach. Feel the breeze on your face and smell the salt in the air.

Request additional anesthetic if you feel pain. You can establish a signal, such as raising your hand, to tell your dentist to stop the procedure. You'll feel more in control of the situation.

A variety of techniques can help you overcome a phobia, like the ones described for the dentist. Mild phobias can often be overcome with support and direct suggestion, including explanation, education, and reassurance. Hypnosis, given in stages, can eliminate a phobia.

Although this is uncomfortable, over-breathing for two or three minutes causes panic attack symptoms to develop and relieves you of the misconception they are induced by a disease or phobic object.

DESENSITIZATION

Visualization and calming self-talk also helps eliminate phobias. List your fears from the most fearful to the least. Start with the least fear on your list. Desensitize that one, and work up the list to the most fearful.

Desensitization involves disconnecting the association of fright from the phobic situation or object. There are several methods used for desensitization. One of the most common is described below.

Relax as deeply as you can and go to your *safe place*. Then visualize being in the phobic situation. Be conscious of your breathing, making sure it is sustained, slow, even breathing from your diaphragm. If you start to get anxious, picture a scene you associate with relaxation. When you feel more relaxed, visualize the phobic situation again. You might expose yourself to little parts of the phobic situation at first. If you're afraid to drive, then imagine you're sitting in the car in the driveway, for example.

Use your creativity, and imagine the phobic situation or object in different colors, sizes, or shapes. You can reduce most, if not all, of the anticipatory anxiety using visualizations. The deeper you relax, the better and faster it goes. Picture yourself smiling as you approach the phobic object. Create visualizations of overcoming the phobia.

Daily visualizations for twenty to thirty minutes at a time are most helpful. The energy from them has accumulative effect, and can turn into enormous power. It may take up to three weeks of visualizing to notice the effect. Imagery desensitization reduces anxiety sufficiently to make the task of real-life desensitization possible.

Use calming self-talk to encourage yourself. "I am one step closer to my goal—free of phobias." "I release the negative fear energy and replace it with positive gentle calmness." "I feel serene and relaxed."

Eliminating phobic objects that symbolize unconscious conflicts usually requires the assistance of a therapist. Bill came for therapy because he couldn't go into his bathroom. He was afraid of the pipes. They triggered such fear that he became momentarily disassociated. He'd fly into a rage and threaten to kill anyone around. Bill had a high pitched voice, many feminine mannerisms and had never married. "I think I'm the only twenty-seven year old male virgin alive. And I'm not homosexual," he quickly added. "I'm just absolutely scared to death of women."

"It's my mother, damn her. Every time I think of a woman, a picture of my mother flashes in my mind. Sometimes I think I'm going crazy. I can't go to the bathroom because I'm afraid of the pipes. So I sneak around behind my apartment building and go in the bushes. That's crazy!"

"Maybe not," I said. "Tell me more about the pipes, and anything else that comes to your mind."

"They're dirty, I . . . I feel my anger rising, I feel so mad I could kill someone. The lamp," he screamed looking at the lamp in my office, "it's turned into a pipe." Suddenly he swung his arm and knocked it over, and picked up the ash tray and threw it across the room.

"What's the matter, Bill?" I asked in as calm a voice as I could muster.

"My God. Why does my mother's face keep looking at me?" Bill was back in reality now, but his momentary disassociation had been frightening.

When Bill came for his next session, he apologized for losing control. "You know, I was in a rage, and nothing could stop me until I heard your voice. I'm really sorry, but in a way it was a giant breakthrough. I had a dream that night, and I remembered what happened to me when I was little." Bill looked at the floor. "I'm going to try to get this out without going off the deep end." He took a breath, shaking his head. "My mother," his voice trailed off, "used to play with my penis in the bathtub. I'm so mad I could kill her." He hit the arm of the chair several times. "I looked at the bathroom pipes while she played with me," Bill wept. "I almost wish I was still afraid of the pipes. I didn't know how much violence and rage I had inside me."

"Bill, you can work through that, like everything else. You're doing good recalling your sexual abuse."

Bill had identified with the source of his sexual violation, fear of, and his rage and anger toward his mother. As he worked through those feelings, to Bill's surprise, his voice became lower. His feminine mannerisms disappeared, and he developed a masculine image. His walk took on an air of confidence. Bill became comfortable in different situations and the panic attacks stopped. He started dating women. A year later he married. Ten years later Bill wrote me a letter and said he and his wife were expecting their second child, and he had had no further problems.

Bill's phobia directly related to his childhood abuse. Other people may have multiple phobias for different reasons. If you have many fears, it's important to lay a plan of action. The task often seems overwhelming, and safer to stay as you are. But by learning how to set limits and priorities, you'll be surprised how fast you'll feel better. Following these simple guidelines starts you on your road to recovery.

PLAN OF ACTION TO OVERCOME FEARS

1. Identify your fears. As one man put it, "I'm afraid of everything." Even if that's the way you feel, don't let it stop you. The practice of writing your fears down helps you focus on the task at hand. If you're afraid of the grocery store, write that down, for example.

2. Categorize your fears. What do they have in common? How many of your fears relate to abandonment? How many relate to having another panic attack? How many relate to what people think of you, loss of love or acceptance? Those might be issues for you to work through. Have they generalized, for example,

from a knife to all sharp objects? By dividing them into groups, you can tackle them, one at a time.

3. Examine your early family history. Did a significant person in your life die or become seriously ill as you were growing up? Were you overprotected or overcontrolled? What were the attitudes in your family regarding being alone? Doing things on your own? Ask your family what happened during your childhood.

Perhaps you were afraid of being alone as a child. That's often a sign you were afraid of losing love and protection. If you discover unresolved grief issues, it's very important to deal with them.

4. Grieving may resolve much of your fear and anxiety. Write a letter to the person you're mourning and explain how you feel. Later, you may burn the letters in a funeral pyre, symbolically releasing them, or create and design your own ritual. Some people go through an actual funeral service. Before you go to sleep at night, say a prayer and ask the Divine for guidance and healing in your dreams.

Other ways to release someone from the past include going to your *safe place* (Described in Chapter 12). Visualize the person you've been mourning. Imagine you are together again. Say all the things you've held back. Continue to do this visualization for twenty minutes at a time until all the emotion is gone. Then that work is complete.

5. List the ways you feel inadequate. Often, phobics feel unprepared to take their place in the world. Do you feel able to make a living? Do you feel skilled at social interactions? Whatever you put down, analyze it logically. You might ask a friend to read your list and discuss it with you. Discover where the feelings come from. If you actually are inadequate in some way, take the necessary courses to develop the skills you need.

Often, your feelings of inadequacy stem from your childhood. Parents who have high expectations and perfectionistic standards create a sense of inadequacy in their children who can never reach their excessively high goals.

When you grow up, you may adopt those same unrealistic expectations. This type of problem is extremely common in dysfunctional homes where a parent was alcoholic. Unrealistic perfectionistic goals and expectations can cause fear.

If any of your expectations are unrealistic, then reset them to something within your limits. This may sound easy, but it's not. You probably have automatic triggers which you react to without thinking. Journaling is an especially important tool for creating change.

When you journal daily, ask yourself, "Did I react to my old unrealistic expectations today?" If you did, write it down. Then write how you plan to correct it the next time it comes around. As an extra bonus, visualize the correction so your subconscious can identify and implement the changes you desire.

6. Realize others have their own agenda. Since most phobics are self-conscious, they often take things personally. If someone makes a rude comment to you, it probably doesn't have anything to do with you. How you think about yourself is what matters. Affirm your positive traits.

When you allow others to effect you by their judgements, you let them set the standards for your life. Take back your power. Analyze where your self-esteem and self-worth come from. How do you feel about yourself? How do you deal with problems? Learn to treat yourself like a beloved friend. You are worthy. It's your birthright.

7. It's time to confront your fears in real-life. Don't think you have to confront them immediately and overwhelm yourself. Again, start with the weakest fear on your list, eliminate that

one, and go on to the next weakest fear. Perhaps you simply need a little encouragement to confront it. When you do, you'll feel more confident. A good time to begin real-life exposure is approximately two to three weeks after you started desensitization by visualization, and are about half way up your list.

If you're confined to the bedroom, then confront the hall. Stand in it from one to three hours. Your anxiety will peak and gradually fade away. Most panic attacks have a duration of fifteen to twenty minutes, with forty-five minutes to come down from the effects. This is the time it takes to trigger the *flight or fight* response, and dissipate the adrenaline in the body. If you're afraid to drive your car, then sit in it for an hour each day, until you're ready to start driving. Whatever you're least afraid of, confront it from one to three hours at a time. After you conquer it, then go to the next least fearful situation.

After exposure to the dreaded situation or object a panic attack may be triggered, but then it subsides. You can relax in that situation and are no longer afraid. The exposure may need repeating several times, so you are reassured there is nothing to fear.

Realize that what you're actually afraid of is not the grocery store or your hall or your car. It's your own feelings you're trying to escape. Those fearful situations or objects were simply there when you had a panic attack or trauma and became sensitized by association to them.

NEURO-LINGUISTIC PROGRAMMING (NLP) PHOBIA REMOVAL TECHNIQUE

Other desensitization methods includes the Neuro-Linguistic Programming Phobia Removal Technique. Utilizing this method, the therapist first asks you to relax and imagine being somewhere else, such as in a movie theater watching the screen. The disassociation helps you to gain distance from overwhelming emotions and stay in control while the process takes place.

Then you are asked to remember good thoughts and feelings from times in your life when you felt strong and secure. If you can't remember any, then you would be asked to imagine a time in the future when you would feel in control.

The therapist uses a light touch on your arm to anchor these good "in control" feelings. Several good feelings may be anchored, one on top of the other to multiply the effect of the positive anchor. Next the fear response is elicited by asking you to see yourself on the movie screen in a situation you are phobic about. That feeling is then anchored on your other arm.

The therapist tests the anchors by touching them, making sure that the "good" feeling is stronger than the phobic response feeling.

If the "good" feeling is weaker, then the therapist continues to illicit "good" feelings, anchoring them one on top of the other. The negative fear response can be spread out in several different anchors along the forearm to minimize it.

Then the therapist holds both anchors (both negative and positive). A heat rash across the top of the forehead, along with some redness and confusion, may occur while both anchors are being touched simultaneously. However, this may not be the only reaction. Other parts of the body may also emit a reaction as the integration occurs. Repressed body memories from abuse and trauma have also surfaced during this process.

The process is completed when only the good feeling is left on the positive anchor and the feeling is gone on the negative anchor. The heat rash and all confusion disappear. If multiple negative anchors are used, do the same process by touching the one powerful positive anchor and each of the negative ones. Integrate them one at a time by holding both anchors until the negative feeling is gone and only the positive one remains.

When the process is finished, the next step is to go to the phobic object and test the results. All fear should be gone. If any fear remains while you are exposed to the phobic object, then the process needs to be repeated.

Phobias vanish suddenly using this technique. You can do all the things you previously limited yourself from doing. If a phobia reoccurs, it's a sign that unconscious conflicts are still being played out, or that in some way you are getting *secondary gains* from it (a woman who develops agoraphobia wants her husband constantly by her side so he can't be with someone else).

PHIL

Phil is a college professor who became phobic about riding elevators. When he stepped inside one, sweat beaded across his forehead and he became dizzy. He thought he might faint. During therapy, he was put into a state of deep relaxation where he realized that he wanted to have an affair.

At the college where he taught, many young coeds attracted his attention. It was in the elevator where he desired to put his hand out and touch one of the young women. Phil over ate to make himself unattractive to further protect himself from breaking his marital bonds.

New coping skills, such as imagining a giant **STOP** sign in his head when he had an impulse to touch a coed, helped Phil. Several anchors dissolved his fear about riding in elevators. Six months later Phil called to say he had lost forty pounds and that he was comfortable riding in elevators.

PARADOXICAL INTENTION THERAPY

Another method helpful for the treatment of panic attacks and phobias is paradoxical intention therapy. It requires the assistance of a therapist.

If you were afraid you would faint if you went to the mall, your therapist would say, "Go ahead and faint." Whatever you feared, your therapist would instruct you to do the opposite of what you would be inclined. If you are instructed to "Go ahead and faint," you try and faint. After several attempts, you discover that you are unable to faint, and your anxiety diminishes.

You are then instructed to repeat this same procedure in selected settings until you experience little or no anxiety. You are instructed to go to the least feared situation first, and allow yourself to become anxious without attempting to interfere with the anxiety.

If you want to avoid the situation physically (by leaving) or cognitively (by imagining being somewhere else), you are to concentrate on making your anxiety worse. If the anxiety intensifies and the usual symptoms of tightness in the chest, sweating, and shortness of breath occur, you are to exaggerate those symptoms as much as possible.

This is the premise of paradoxical intention. You are requested to do the opposite of what you might be naturally inclined to do (i.e., avoid the attacks). Deliberately intensifying the symptoms eventually reduces the anxiety and weakens the attack. When you discover you're unable to exaggerate the attack, the anxiety and panic sensations diminish significantly.

Although paradoxical intention may eliminate panic symptoms in some cases, it does not always focus on underlying issues that contribute to panic attacks (marital problems, interpersonal difficulties or incest).

Sometimes your fears are symbols of unfinished business: identity issues, separation issues, anger issues. If you're not in touch with your feelings, you're stuck. Panic attacks don't really come from out of the blue. There are reasons for them. It's up to you to discover what they are.

Joan came to therapy because she was phobic about driving her car. She had an infant son, didn't work, and depended on her husband for almost everything. Joan liked to please people, and felt it was her duty to please her husband.

She began having panic attacks when she drove her car. While driving, she'd fantasize about not going home, driving to faraway places and having affairs with strangers. Then a panic attack would strike. She stopped driving her car because she feared having more panic attacks.

Joan didn't know how to talk to her husband about what was wrong in the marriage. She wished something magical would happen to help her escape the situation.

In therapy she learned how to talk about her feelings and discuss them with her husband. Joan developed an identity of her own, and stopped the people pleasing. But best of all, she stopped having panic attacks. Joan could drive the car again. And the marriage improved.

INNER CHILD WORK

Inner child work is especially healing, and helps develop a new vitalized sense of self-hood. I recommend at least a year of diligent effort on inner child work. It's certainly not a quick fix, but it lasts, and you'll overcome many insecurities.

To contact your inner child, go to your *safe place.* See yourself as both an adult and as a very young child. You may want to visualize another person with you such as a spiritual leader, or ask your higher self to send you a guide.

Then, for twenty to thirty minutes twice a week, go to your *safe place* and comfort your inner child. Ask your inner child how you can help. Allow your inner child to lead you into the areas of your life that need healing. This inspirational process helps heal the child within. All areas of your life improve when you reclaim the strength and power of your child.

SETTING GOALS

Set goals and be specific when working toward extinguishing your phobias. Instead of aiming for "being comfortable when I go out," set a specific goal such as "going to the store and buying an item I want." Establish a time frame to accomplish the goal and make a commitment to stick with it.

Realize you're actually not afraid of the grocery store or the hall or your car. It's your own feelings you've been trying to escape. Those situations or objects were simply there when you had a panic attack or trauma and you became sensitized by association to them. Nothing works better than facing fears directly. Once you've fully desensitized yourself from the phobic situations and objects in real life, you may remain free of fear only until you have another panic attack. You may continue to develop more phobias of places and situations where new attacks occur, and have to start all over again. To be totally free of the phobias, the inner conflicts need to be resolved.

CHAPTER 12

PSYCHIC TRAUMA

Tina sobbed, "I feel like ice water is running through my veins." Her long silky brown hair cascaded around her face as she stared at her wedding ring. "It's horrible. I can't stop shaking. I won't leave my home. I don't answer the telephone. And at night, when I can sleep, I have nightmares." Tina lived in a state of perpetual shock. "I know it's the coward's way out, but suicide often seems like an answer," she said. "If I'm going to live feeling like this, what's the use?"

As her story unfolded, Tina explained how she and her husband had experienced severe financial problems for several years. Then, one day, returning home from work, she walked into her bedroom to find her husband had shot himself in the head. Blood had splattered all over the walls, pictures, curtains, the bed and carpet. It was a scene she'd remember the rest of her life.

"Why didn't he tell me he was thinking about suicide?" she cried. "We could have worked things out. Instead, he leaves me a note, and tells me exactly what to do with the money." Her body shook uncontrollably. "The money. He killed himself so the kids and I would have his insurance money. I loved him," she trembled. "I wanted him alive. Bankruptcy. We could have lived through it. But instead, he details how to save the house, and pay off the bills. He's trying to talk to me from the grave."

Tiny seizures shivered through Tina as she talked. Her brain didn't transmit messages to the body effectively. She'd forget what she was saying in the middle of a sentence, or walk into a room and forget why she went there. Her body felt cold, as if the life force was gone.

A deep depression permeated her life. When she came for treatment, her husband had been dead for several months. The financial problems, continuous stress and her husband's violent suicide had escalated into what seemed insurmountable tragedy for Tina.

Her mind couldn't accept what happened because she couldn't understand it. Tina's psychic trauma cut her to the core. None of her regular defenses worked. She had difficulty falling and staying asleep. She couldn't concentrate. Flashbacks plagued her. She startled easily. She'd go from tears to outbursts of anger in a single sentence.

"I feel so helpless and powerless. I walk around like a zombie. I can't understand why he did it. We always talked things over.

And then he decides to take his life and leave me all alone," Tina cried. She rolled up into a tiny ball in the overstuffed chair and rocked like an infant. It was the first time she had tried to comfort herself.

"You need to nurture yourself a lot now," I said.

"I feel raw. A neighbor came over and took Kenneth's things out of the house. She said it would be better if I didn't look at them. But I miss him. I need his things.

People think they're helping, but they're not." The more she rocked, the more she calmed down. Her shivers had almost stopped when suddenly, she burst into tears again. Her entire body jerked.

"It comes in waves," I said. "Don't fight it. Go with the feelings. The shivers will get fewer and farther apart with time, and finally stop." Tina shook her head, yes, she understood.

Several days later Tina burst into my office. "I'm really angry at Kenneth. He had no right to do that to me. All this time I've been feeling helpless about it, but now I'm mad. Getting angry gives me a sense of power. He really betrayed me. All the trust I put in him. He was my life. I never made any decisions on my own. I always waited for his approval. I wouldn't even pick out a color to paint the kitchen by myself. I'd ask him what he wanted. Now, I'm all alone."

"You're getting some perspective on what's happened. Now is a good time to explore who you are. What do you want for yourself?" I said. "This can be a new beginning."

"Yes. Part of me wants that, and part of me still wants Kenneth back. I think of him as being alive. I can't bury him in my mind, not yet.

His betrayal makes me fearful. I hope he's up there looking down on all this and knows how much he hurt me. It's not fair," Tina said with tears in her eyes.

"I still can't go into our bedroom without seeing blood everywhere. The flashback I have most is the housekeeper cleaning the blood out of the carpet. It took her all day. The house we fought so hard to keep, and Kenneth died for, I've decided to sell. Isn't that ironic," she laughed bitterly. "I can't stand the memories."

Over the next few months Tina grieved. Then one day she walked into my office and announced, "I'm moving to Colorado. It's time to start a new life." Her eyes still reflected the anger and pain from her loss.

"You sound angry, and your eyes look like you've been crying a lot," I said. "Are you finished with the past and ready to make a major move?"

"Yes. I'm angry at Kenneth for leaving me, but I'm not helpless. I'm not stupid. I can make it on my own. I'm sorry he chose the way he did, but I've got to go on with my life." Her hand curled into a fist over her heart. "I may always feel this void in my heart, this emptiness where Kenneth was. But at last I can forgive him. I'm free to start again."

POST TRAUMATIC STRESS DISORDER

Post traumatic stress disorder occurs when a sudden, unexpected, shocking event or series of blows assaults you. You probably won't become fully traumatized unless you feel utterly helpless during the incident or situations. Trying not to think about the trauma is a common defense, but the more you suppress it, the more flashbacks you'll have.

Post traumatic stress disorder symptoms last for more than a month and are characterized by:

- difficulty falling or staying asleep

- irritability or outbursts of anger
- difficulty concentrating
- hypervigilance
- exaggerated startle response
- flashbacks
- physiologic reactivity upon exposure to events that symbolize or resemble an aspect of the traumatic event (a woman raped on a stairwell breaks out in a sweat every time she sees a stairwell)
- recurrent distressing dreams of the event
- inability to recall an important aspect of the trauma
- feeling of detachment or estrangement from others
- unable to have loving feelings
- sense of a foreshortened future (does not expect to have a career, marriage, or children, or a long life)
- markedly diminished interest in significant activities

ABNORMAL BRAIN WAVES

The emotional recovery from post traumatic stress disorder is complicated by other problems. Brain rhythms, the electrical impulses associated with states of attention and consciousness, become abnormal. They are popularly called brain waves because they are recorded as "waves" on graph paper (the electroencephalographic record or EEG).

There are four major brain rhythms

The *beta rhythm* is associated with active thinking or active attention. In beta the attention is focused on the outside world or problem-solving.

The *alpha rhythm* is associated with a relaxed, internally focused state with closed eyes. The mind is alert but at ease and not focused on external processes or engaged in organized, analytical, or problem-solving thinking. It's the state you pass through as you drift to sleep and wake up.

The *theta rhythm* is usually associated with drowsy or semi-unconscious states. It appears as consciousness slips toward unawareness and is often accompanied by hypnagogic (dreamlike) images.

A fourth frequency band, the *delta rhythm*, is primarily associated with deep sleep.

HYPERVIGILANT

When you have a post traumatic stress disorder, you're vigilant. The alpha brain waves become diminished and produce waves of poor quality. You can't relax or drift off to sleep. When you do sleep, it's light and you frequently jerk awake. Your attention is riveted on the external world, scanning for the next danger or attack, either real or imagined. Your senses are hyper-alert. The immune and digestive systems are depressed. As the body's stored up supplies of energy are used up, stress and fatigue set in. You run on raw adrenaline.

CHEMICAL CHANGES

Continuous stress causes chemical changes in the body. The brain's neurotransmitters that transmit information to the body become inoperable or inefficient and the natural opiates for fighting pain and stresses become overtaxed. That means you can't concentrate and frequently forget what's on your mind. You may have craving for food, drugs or alcohol. A deep depression usually sets in. Once you learn to relax your body and mind, you start healing. But it may take the neurotransmitters up to two years to recover once the damage is done.

VULNERABILITY TO POST TRAUMATIC STRESS DISORDER

Women who have been raped; children who have been emotionally, physically, or sexually abused; anyone who has lived in a home where violence occurred; anyone who has witnessed a violent crime or bloody accident; and even patients who are unprepared for surgery are subject to it. Also, drinking heavily or taking drugs for any length of time may cause a post traumatic stress disorder.

Extreme stress can cause a breakthrough of repressed memories into consciousness and trigger a panic attack. Ironically, if your life calms down and everything seems to be going well—then the unconscious may open up. Relaxation causes flashbacks and breakthroughs of repressed memories.

Lou had moved to the mountains with her husband to retire and enjoy the winter sports. She was fifty, had reared two daughters, and thought her life was together. Then suddenly panic attacks struck. Bizarre thoughts of suicide entered her mind. She described the past five years as the most painful in her life as memories of her childhood incest emerged.

ATTEMPTS TO SELF-MEDICATE

Attempts at self-medicating post traumatic stress disorder can cause addictions. You may drink alcohol or take drugs or have sex to ease the stress. The more you indulge, the more ineffective that becomes, so the more you grasp a quick fix. Then you're caught in a downward spiral.

Couples who have had a rocky relationship for several years, and even business and financial struggles are enough to cause a post traumatic stress disorder. A divorce, or any situation that suddenly changes your entire life can result in this disorder.

Not everyone gets a post traumatic stress disorder. If you can accept what happened and deal with it gradually, you may overcome the trauma.

But most people deny or suppress the trauma, especially if it happens in childhood when coping resources are few. Then, suddenly, years later, feelings of panic, fear, and nightmares may erupt.

LIFE STYLE DISORDER

Some people develop a chaotic life style as a defense from internal conflicts. They can't contain or process their own internal pain so they project it onto their environment by creating crises. They go from crisis to crisis, because that keeps their attention focused on the immediacy of their problems. A bad marriage or relationship can serve the same purpose, and although there may be pain and suffering, you at least know what's troubling you, you think.

Addictions (alcohol, drugs, relationships, sex, running), and even a continuous struggle with your weight, exerts enough focused energy away from your internal pain and chaos to allow you to ignore it.

This pattern can become a life-style disorder. It's not what you remember that bothers you. It's what you don't, won't, and can't remember. Your life in the external world often reflects a mirror image of what you're repressing in your internal world and the unconscious.

KAREN

Karen thought she had her life together. She was married and had three school age children. But out of the blue she began having panic attacks when she was thirty-five. She was hospitalized four times that year. She was treated with drugs, and finally shock treatments. No one could figure out what was wrong. Then it surfaced. Her father had used her for sex games when she was a child. When she had developed the strength to say "No" to him, he physically beat her.

When she came to me for counseling, Karen suffered from panic attacks and a serious depression. Now it was time to comfort her inner child, her traumatized self, heal the incest, pain, anger, shame, and grieve her lost childhood.

LOSS OF SENSE OF SELF

Loss of the sense of self happens when you are permanently changed by traumatic incidents such as sexual abuse or parental snatchings.

You still live with your remembrances of an old, normally functioning self. You need to grieve the loss because a part of you died.

The effects of trauma from childhood can be found in attitudes and fears which persist into adulthood: long-standing superstitions, fascination with horror books and movies, and fear of fear. Childhood traumas do not seem to "fade away," as once thought.

If you uncover a traumatic experience from your childhood, it's best to talk it out with a nonjudgmental friend or therapist. Be sure and go at your own pace. If you try to do too much too fast, you may become overwhelmed.

Recovery may take years. As you develop the ability to cope with the situation, the trauma will resolve itself. Don't force anything, but allow the healing to take place naturally. Like mending a wounded heart, give yourself the nurturing, love, and understanding you needed at the time you were traumatized to promote the healing. Reassure yourself daily that you are healing and becoming whole.

SAFE PLACE

An especially important technique to learn is how to create a *safe place.* People who have been abused or traumatized don't have a place they feel safe inside themselves. They're cut to the very heart of their soul. And because they feel hurt and betrayed, they won't trust others. This leads to isolation and loneliness.

Steve attended a workshop I gave. When it came time to do an inner journey, I asked the participants to go to their *safe place.* Steve left the room. Later I found him standing in a corner. He said he didn't have a *safe place* inside himself, and it scared him.

Steve told me about his long history of child abuse. I explained to him how to create a *safe place.* When he was able to do this, he was very proud and told his therapist about his *safe place.* The therapist told Steve to imagine his therapy office as his *safe place*. Steve had been abused again, by his possessive therapist who didn't allow him to have a *safe place* of his own.

After you create your *safe place,* don't let anyone take it away from you. It's yours. You can make a *safe place* inside yourself by following these simple instructions.

Close your eyes and focus your attention on the space between your nose. Quiet the mind and body. Keep your muscles still as possible. To relax, take five fast, very deep, even breathes from the diaphragm. Then, on the exhalation of each breath after that, count consecutively from ten to one. On the first breath, think ten to yourself as you exhale. On the next breath, think nine as you exhale, and so on until you get to one.

Roll your eyes up as far as you can. Imagine you can look up through the top of your head. Then slowly lower your eyelids while you are looking up. After your eyes are closed, focus them on the spot between your eyebrows.

When you feel relaxed, begin to image a room and decorate it with furniture, paint or paper the walls, and do all the things to it you would do to a regular room. Put pictures on the walls, and a favorite chair in the room for you to relax in. The point is that it becomes a place where you feel safe. Some people like to imagine a place in nature—a setting by a mountain lake or a sandy beach, for example.

Then see yourself, feel yourself, and hear yourself relaxed in your safe place. Do this for at least twenty to thirty minutes each day. You may visualize walking on a beach, or hiking in the mountains to deepen the relaxation.

When images start to appear on their own, simply observe what happens without trying to analyze or think about it. Mental focused activity brings you out of the deeper state of relaxation. Impressions may also come in the form of feelings, or you may hear a voice or sounds.

This is a process, and each day when you do this exercise, you'll relax a little deeper. But it may take six or seven relaxation periods to relax deep enough to feel you're getting anywhere. Your conscious mind needs to relearn its okay to let go, and relax. When you do let go and relax, it becomes easier to relax all during the day. As you relax, you may feel your body suddenly jerk and tense up again. Reassure yourself that you are safe. Eventually you will be able to stay relaxed. You now have created a *safe place* to give you a sense of security and an inner resource to draw upon.

NORMALIZING BRAIN WAVES

As you relax, and go very, very, deep, notice that you experience an objectivity about your body. You may see hypnagogic images flash before you.

This is the point where alpha waves deepen into theta waves. This is a state of deepest relaxation, and necessary to achieve for the alpha waves to return to normal. It's like pushing the reset button on a piece of machinery that's blown a fuse and stopped functioning. When you go into this deep state of relaxation, you are pushing your mental reset button so your body can normalize itself.

This crossover from alpha to theta brain wave activity is called reverie. The terminology used in describing the reverie state varies from calling it the "fringe" of consciousness, the "preconscious," the "transliminal mind," "twilight state," to "transcendence."

If you go into reverie thirty minutes a day, five days a week for six weeks, your stress level can lower and your body can normalize. Your neuroreceptors may begin to heal, and your brain waves can return to normal. If you've used alcohol to help cope with your symptoms, stop drinking. Once the alpha waves become normalized, you may find you'll get sick if you drink. In Chapter 13, reverie and brain waves will be discussed in more depth.

In the reverie state you feel emotionally detached from whatever you see. Any conflicts from your earliest childhood through adulthood may appear in hypnagogic (dream like) imagery. These images have been described as "more vivid," and "more realistic," than dreams, and they "come and go in a flash," and "contained detailed material which I didn't know I knew." The images become foggy a session or two prior to the release of very sensitive traumatic material. Seek a professional therapist or support system to help you process what comes up.

Traumatic repressed memories and childhood events are recorded in the hypothalamus region in the brain. This area has been referred to as a computer with "write only" programs. Some scientists speculate the "write only" programs were designed for survival during man's prehistoric era, but are no longer suited for today's complex societies.

When you are in reverie, the door opens not only to read these "write only" programs, but to rewrite them as well. Reverie is also used to ask questions and receive answers, solve problems, receive inspiration, and develop creativity. When I have gone into reverie, I have also seen images of places I would go in the future and the people I would meet there.

Going into reverie as a daily routine is known to enhance health and promote an overall sense of well-being. Obtaining reverie is an advanced technique. The biggest challenge is to stay awake while you are in reverie. Ironically, falling asleep can also be an effort to avoid confrontation with your unconscious.

The chief thing to remember when doing deep relaxation is to *let go*. Do not become emotionally involved with what you see, or try and figure out what the images are telling you. The hypnagogic (dream like) images are very fragile and quickly forgotten. As soon as you come out of reverie, write your impressions down as fast as you can. Then process whatever came up. A professional counselor can be very helpful to you in assisting you in deep relaxation and processing. More information on deep relaxation plus tips to remember images are included in Chapter 13.

Because of the extreme pressure and stress caused by a post traumatic stress disorder, many of the vitamins and minerals in your body may be leached out. Watch your diet, and make sure it's loaded with nutrients. Allow yourself extra rest, relaxation and exercise to help your body rebuild and become healthy and strong again. A vacation or break in your routine may be helpful.

MASS POST TRAUMATIC STRESS DISORDER

Anyone can be subjected to a post traumatic stress disorder and panic attacks given the right set of circumstances. In 1938, a radio broadcast of H.G. Wells, *The War of the Worlds*, led thousands to believe that an interplanetary conflict had started with invading Martians spreading death and destruction in New Jersey and New York.

Hundreds of people fled from the fictional Martian hordes, and large numbers of adults required medical treatment for shock and hysteria. But in a panic situation, adrenaline, not reason, becomes the motor power governing behavior.

Many times, it's your perception of what happened instead of what actually happened that causes the trauma. War veterans who have had a post traumatic stress disorder report they often feel guilty and responsible for a buddy who died, or for what they did. But when they go into the reverie state and observe what actually did happen, they usually find there was nothing different they could have done. Then they are able to accept it and go on with their lives.

That's what getting over post traumatic stress disorder is all about. Learning to accept what happened, integrate it, forgive the trauma, or abuse, pain and anger. Then *let it go.*

CHAPTER 13

EXERCISE & RELAXATION

Jennifer cried, "I'm not going to exercise today. I'm too depressed. Besides, I'm afraid exercise might trigger another panic attack." Jennifer lay in her hospital bed and looked out the window. She had been admitted to the psychiatric ward for panic attacks. She seldom took part in the ward's activities. Jennifer felt like a helpless victim and had become increasingly passive, afraid to do anything for fear of having another panic attack.

Many people who have panic attacks may feel helpless and powerless and take a passive role in life because they feel victimized by their illness. If you feel this way, you may not want to exercise. But exercise helps. While the old saying, "When in doubt, run in circles, scream and shout," may seem irrational, it's not. Exercise helps to discharge the pent up energy brought on by the *flight or fight* response, and gives you a sense of doing something.

If you walk less than two and one half miles per day doing your usual routine of slow walking, working, house cleaning and shopping, you are considered inactive.

Consult your physician before beginning an exercise program. Your doctor may recommend a program of restricted or supervised exercise appropriate to your needs. Very sensitive people can trigger a panic attack by attempting vigorous exercise when they're not used to it.

SODIUM LACTATE

Studies show that subjects prone to panic attacks, when given sodium lactate, usually have a panic attack. But normal subjects, when given sodium lactate, seldom do.

Sodium lactate is normally secreted by the body during vigorous exercise. It's what makes your muscles sore after a hard workout.

A good walk is better to start with initially. Because regular exercise oxygenates (oxygen turnover in the body) the blood and brain, it helps increase alertness and concentration as well as oxidizes substances it doesn't need, including lactic acid. So moderate exercise is important to begin with. Build up slowly, over time, to good, strenuous exercise. Then any increase in lactic acid will be offset by your body's increased ability to handle it.

EXERCISE TO REDUCE STRESS

Exercise is one of the simplest and most effective means of stress reduction. It's also an excellent way to relieve chronic muscular tension, spasms, tics and tremors. You can improve your cardiovascular efficiency, metabolism and develop endurance with regular aerobic exercise such as fast walking, jogging or jumping on a small trampoline. Cross country skiing is the most strenuous aerobic exercise. But any kind of continuous exercise gives the desired effect as long as it's maintained for twenty minutes so the heart has a good workout.

Avoid exercising once a week. Doing infrequent spurts of vigorous exercise is stressful to your body and may do more harm than good. Exercise three times a week for twenty minutes is sufficient.

Your heart is strengthened and enlarged, your blood vessels become more elastic, and your oxygen utilization becomes more efficient. You can reduce your chances of developing high blood pressure, heart attacks, strokes, and panic attacks by regular exercise.

HATHA YOGA

Hatha Yoga is a form of exercise you can do all your life. It is composed of a series of body postures and certain breathing exercises. The postures release blocked emotional energy in the body and open up channels for meditation. The bending and stretching exercises increase your overall flexibility. Yoga helps stabilize the emotions and elevate your mental attitude. It is a holistic approach to the well-being of your entire system—leading to a oneness in body, mind, and spirit.

An awareness of your life path and purpose may be revealed to you while sitting quietly in a pose. There are many excellent books on yoga with pictures of the postures. Classes are also an excellent way to learn the postures.

According to yoga philosophy, a person who looks up is looking at the future, looking straight ahead is in the present, and looking down is in the past.

While Hatha Yoga offers lifelong flexibility, competitive sports such as tennis develop strength. Sports help release aggression, frustration and anger.

By building strength and flexibility into your body, you get a sense of power and a perception that your body works for you, not against you.

MOTIVATION TO EXERCISE

Most people who don't exercise know they need to, but lack motivation. If you start off doing a little exercise, say ten minutes, and then add five more minutes the next day, you get the idea of how invigorating regular exercise can be. If you'll exercise every day, you'll create a space in your life for it and build exercise into a habit. Eventually extend the time to twenty minutes a day. You might look forward to your exercise time, as a way of relieving your tensions and frustrations.

Exercise can reinforce the idea that you're not a helpless victim. You can do something about your situation. And it gives you more energy.

Exercise helps the body function better. It improves circulation, digestion, metabolism, elimination and reduces anxiety, depression, insomnia. If you're afraid exercise may harm you, a visit to your doctor for an evaluation can put those fears aside.

Exercise or yoga classes may help if you have difficulty sticking to a regular exercise program. Classes are also a way of meeting people if you've become socially isolated.

Relaxation techniques are very helpful in reducing fear and anxiety. When you combine regular exercise with a program of deep relaxation and meditation, you increase your chances of overcoming panic attacks.

PROPER BREATHING

Proper breathing is an important aspect of relaxing. Watch a baby breathe from the abdomen. Babies are naturally relaxed. A simple test to determine where you're breathing is to place one hand on your chest and one hand on your abdomen. Which hand moves?

People who are anxious and fearful breathe high in their chest. When they gasp for air, a process called reverse thoracic breathing begins. These light shallow, rapid breaths are called hyperventilation. Hyperventilation may trigger a panic attack.

Learning to redirect the breath to deep, slow, diaphragm breathing stops many of the limited symptoms and panic attacks. If you've been doing reverse thoracic breathing, diaphragm breathing may feel strange. Remind yourself to pay attention to your breath, and redirect it in a kind, gentle manner, to slow down, and breathe from your diaphragm.

SAM

When Sam came for therapy, he had already made several suicide attempts. Unable to work because of panic attacks and depression, he spent most of his days in bed. I noticed he breathed light shallow breaths and called that to his attention.

"I've always breathed this way, all my life," he replied. "I'm a frightened little rabbit." This seemed an unusual self-image comment coming from such a large man.

"It would be better to shift your breathing down to your abdomen, and stop pushing the panic button."

"But I've always been this way. I can't change," he protested.

Sam had a strong polarity response (he took the opposite viewpoint of whatever was presented to him). Before his session was over, Sam had told me his life story and the relentless depression and panic that paralyzed him. He couldn't relax, even though most of his day was spent lying in bed trying to escape his terrible symptoms.

Sam had suffered many losses and traumatic events in his youth. First, he was taken away from his parents at age four and placed in a foster home. Then his father had murdered his mother, but was never convicted. Next his foster mother, to whom he had gotten attached, died. A gang of older boys sexually abused Sam repeatedly when he was six. His life didn't get much better when he was a teenager. He had angrily confronted his father about his mother's death. His father told him about the murder. Soon after, his father died.

Sam looked at me with tearful eyes and said, "See, I have too much pain to deal with. And pain is all I have. I'm nothing. I can't work. I can't do anything, except wait to die."

"You can do something about your panic attacks," I said.

"What?" he asked defiantly.

"You can start by lowering your breathing to your abdomen, and give your body a rest from the panic attacks. Deep relaxation will enable you to release some of the pain and allow your muscles and neurotransmitters to recover from the chronic stress they're under."

"How do I do that?" Sam asked curiously.

"First, breathe from your diaphragm. Put your hand over your stomach and breathe into your hand."

Sam put his hand on his stomach and attempted a few breaths. "This is weird," he said.

"Yes, it feels strange, because you've done it backwards most of your life. But keep it up, and you'll get used to proper breathing. As you get better, we'll deal with the other painful issues in your life. But right now, you need to build in resources for yourself. Stopping the panic attacks and learning how to relax are resources.

DEEP RELAXATION

Deep relaxation helps reduce panic attacks, depression and chronic stress. The relaxation response is related to skin temperature. When you're anxious, the small vessels close off under the surface of the skin to provide the extra blood supply to the brain, heart, lungs, and large muscles, as in the *fight or flight* response. When this happens, the skin becomes cooler (because of the reduced blood flow). The sayings, "cold hands—warm heart," "white as a sheet" refer to this response.

Relaxation is characterized by slow, deep breathing, slow heart rate, increased digestion, bowel and bladder function, unfocused mental activity and surface (skin) warming.

Relaxation changes blood flow. Since the brain, heart, lungs, and large muscles do not have an increased oxygen demand, the blood supply is reduced to those body parts, and can return to surface areas and digestive tract.

If you're taking medication for high blood pressure or prescription drugs to relax, tell your doctor when you start relaxation exercises. Your medication needs monitoring and can probably be reduced as you develop the ability to relax.

Relaxation can be accomplished in five or six sessions of thirty minutes twice a day, or forty-five minute sessions four times a week.

There are several different methods of relaxation. The simplest of these techniques is to tell your various body parts to relax and be calm and quiet. To begin relaxation training, find a comfortable position and relax your body as much as you can.

Be aware of any remaining tension in your muscles and do what you need to completely relax those muscles

Now that you are relaxed, take five full deep breaths, and then begin to breathe deeply and evenly from your abdomen. Make the in and out breath even and continuous. Do this for several breaths.

Now, on the next breath, as you exhale, close your eyes, and mentally see and repeat the number 3, three times. Trace it in your mind. On the next breath, see and repeat the number 2, three times. Trace it in your mind. Now see and repeat 1, three times on the next breath, and trace it in your mind, three times.

You will begin to experience changes that are associated with your relaxation. Deepen those experiences by slowly counting down from ten to one as you exhale each breath: ten, nine, eight, *deeper*, seven, six, *calmer and deeper*, five, four and three, *deeper and deeper*, two and one.

While you are in a relaxed state, make visual images of your body relaxed. Remember a time from the past when you were totally relaxed and at peace with yourself and your environment. Create that scene in vivid detail. If you can't remember a time when you were relaxed, visualize a time in the future and see yourself totally relaxed in the future situation. Imagine what relaxation feels like.

Because the blood flows away from the extremities during the *flight or fight* response, you might visualize your feet in buckets of warm water. Make your images as vivid and real as possible. Start with your feet. Say, *feet, relax. I feel my feet getting warmer and warmer.* Then move on to your ankles. *Say, ankles, relax. Visualize the relaxation, and imagine what it feels like. Make it real with the power of your mind.*

Take your time and move slowly up your body to your calves. Say, *calves, relax. Knees, relax. Thighs, relax.* Make visual images of each part relaxed. Next, go to your hands. Suggest they are getting warmer and warmer. Make visual images of warming mittens on your hands. Tell your fingers to relax. Then continue to relax your forearms. Say, *forearms, relax. Upper arms, relax. Lower back, relax. Mid back, relax. Shoulders, relax. My shoulders are loose and limp. The relaxation is moving into my neck. Neck relax. My scalp is relaxing. I can feel the relaxation draining down into my face. My eyelids are heavy and relaxed.* Leave a little space between your teeth. Say, *jaw relax. Throat, relax.*

You might prefer to do this exercise at bedtime as a sleep aid. To drift off to sleep, exhale twice as long as you inhale for several breaths. That will cause you to feel tired and sleepy.

Relaxation is progressive when done on a daily basis. Each day you feel more relaxed.

This type of relaxation helps quiet your muscles and tension. Many people record a tape of their own relaxation instructions and listen to it while they relax. Relaxation in itself will help calm your anxiety.

Another type of relaxation routine consists of flexing and relaxing the different muscle groups. This form of relaxation is suggested when stress has become chronic and the muscles are in a suspended state of contraction. Then, the muscles don't know how to relax. They think tension is normal, so they strive to maintain a certain degree of tension. The muscles need retraining.

Do this by flexing and relaxing the different muscle groups, so the muscles can learn the difference between tension and relaxation.

Start with your feet. Flex and relax them. Then take the muscle group from the ankles to the knee, and flex and relax them. The muscles from the knee to the hip, and flex and relax them. Flex and relax the hips. Flex and relax your hands, forearms and upper arms, one muscle group at a time. Flex and relax the muscles in the lower back, abdomen, chest, and then the upper back, shoulders, neck, scalp and face, one muscle group at a time.

In a deep state of relaxation, with your eyes closed, project your body onto a mental view screen. Scan your body, up and down, up and down, looking for signs of any remaining tension. Do what you need to completely and totally relax. If you image any dark or gray areas in your body on your mental view screen, mentally project a golden healing light into those areas. Make it real with the power of your imagination.

You are in a deeper state of relaxation now. Continue the experience, and mentally repeat the following phrases three times to yourself:

I am relaxing . . . . my body. . . . . .completely . . . .
I feel heavy . . . . and warm . . . .all over . . . .
I am calm . . . . peaceful . . . . .and serene . . . .

Repeat the following sentences slowly and with frequent pauses that relate to heaviness and warmth.

- *I am quite relaxed.*
- *My arms and hands feel heavy and warm.*
- *I feel quite quiet.*
- *My whole body is relaxed and my hands are warm.*
- *My hands are warm.*
- *Warmth is flowing into my hands, they are warm.*

• *My hands are warm, relaxed and warm.*

Be aware of any sensations that are a part of your relaxation.

BIOFEEDBACK

A biofeedback hand warming instrument is extremely helpful in attaining a deep level of relaxation. Some are inexpensive and cost about $30.00. A biofeedback instrument has an electric heat sensor probe which attaches to a finger. Some machines make sounds and/or lights flash to indicate if your temperature is going up or down. The temperature of your finger is monitored by the machine and fed back for you to read.

While you deepen the relaxation by making suggestions and visualizations of your hands getting warmer, your hand temperature rises.

You get the best results when you have your hand close to your body.

People who have been traumatized and sexually abused usually have finger temperatures in the seventies. The object is to raise the temperature to ninety-six degrees for ten minutes or longer.

When you can raise your finger temperature to ninety-six degrees, ten minutes or longer for five consecutive days, you're ready to go into reverie.

Reverie is a deep state of relaxation characterized behaviorally by vivid, spontaneous hypnagogic imagery and theta brain rhythms.

Alpha-theta biofeedback brain wave training is highly recommended to achieve this deeper level of relaxation. Anyone who has a post traumatic stress disorder, alcoholism, chronic stress, depression and panic attacks can benefit and reduce their symptoms using this training.

Biofeedback brain wave training is offered in most hospitals, medical centers, and some doctors, social workers and psychologists offer biofeedback training. Utilizing brain wave equipment, electrodes are attached to your head. Earphones beep different tones that indicate if the particular brain wave is beta, alpha, theta, or delta.

BRAIN WAVES

Beta brain wave rhythms are associated with consciousness, attachments and critical thinking. In alpha brain wave rhythms, you are slightly detached and inwardly focused. Alpha brain waves are associated with relaxation. In theta brain wave activity, you are definitely detached, and in touch with your unconscious. You experience reverie, and spontaneous flashes of images. Theta brain waves are usually associated with sleep and dreaming, but with practice, you can stay awake in theta. Delta is associated with deep sleep.

In brain wave training, you listen with your eyes closed to the beeps of the biofeedback machine. You learn to associate your body relaxation with the different tones. It is important to know what your body feels like when it produces alpha and theta brain waves. A test to determine if you're in theta brain wave rhythms is to see yourself, and then look back at yourself. If you can remain totally detached, you're in theta brain wave rhythms—where you want to be. This is the state called reverie.

You naturally go through this state as you drift off to sleep and as you wake up. It is possible for you to get into reverie without a machine hookup. The advantage of a biofeedback instrument is that you definitely know when you're in reverie. The beeps from the machine also help you remember images and stay awake.

To go into reverie after you can warm your hands to ninety-six degrees, close your eyes, let go mentally, be quiet and emotionally calm. Be open and allow it to happen. Keep your body still. Muscle movement will pull you out of reverie. If you try and make it happen, it probably won't. Imagine you're passively observing what happens, avoiding judgments or thinking. You will probably start to feel tired as your mind deepens. Some people focus on the space between the tip of their nose, or the rising and falling of their breath. Continue to be receptive and open.

An image might flash briefly and go away. Don't try to understand it. The next time it may stay longer when it flashes. If you think about it, your thoughts will require alpha or beta brainwaves (conscious thought requires beta brain waves) and you will interrupt the process. If you jar out of reverie, it might take you a long time to get back in it. However, if you have trouble remembering the images, you might hold something like a little ball in your hand. Then, as you drift deeper, you'll drop it and wake up. Write down everything that was on your mind until that moment.

While you are in reverie, hypnagogic (dream like) images appear and visualizations take on a life of their own. Don't analyze them. Later, when you come out of the relaxation state, write down the images you saw. Ask yourself, "What is ______?" (whatever you saw). Theta brain wave activity triggers old memories and feelings. When the memories flash, you will feel detached and protected.

Reverie activates the hypothalamus region of your brain which contains the memories of your childhood and adulthood. Eventually your emotional conflicts will slowly surface for you to deal with, one at a time. Theoretically, the mind does not give you more than you can handle. But later, after you are out of reverie for about fifteen minutes, feelings of grief or sadness may surface and stay with you for several hours, days, or as long as it takes to dissolve that energy. Or that night, you may have a dream that shows you a traumatic event or conflict. This is part of the healing process. You may want the help of a professional therapist to help you process the feelings or the images you see.

Avoid using commercial alpha-theta drivers or simulators to achieve reverie. They give off alpha and theta sound rhythms and can open up the hypothalamus region of the brain before you are ready to handle sensitive material. These types of machines can be dangerous. You will be safe if you do it naturally using the techniques described.

The images you see in reverie get foggy a session or two prior to the release of traumatic material. There is nothing to fear. You don't get the full picture all at once. It comes little by little, in subsequent sessions. You usually don't remember it like it actually happened. One woman who recalled that she was sexually abused at age four, realized she had subsequently felt guilty and responsible for her abuse. Victims, especially children, often feel guilty and responsible for their own traumas.

Once you've recalled the trauma, you'll feel relieved. It's what you repress that hurts you. Once you've remembered traumatic events, you'll probably stop repressing feelings because that's no longer necessary. This in itself is healing.

Some people go so deep into reverie that they are disoriented when they come out of it. You may need to walk around a little while until you get all the way back into beta brain waves. Don't attempt to drive a car until you're sure you're all the way back into beta consciousness.

For maximum results, go into the reverie state at least twenty to thirty minutes, five times a week, for six weeks to elicit the healing process. The healing process involves not only retrieving lost memories, but normalizing brain wave patterns and revitalizing brain neurotransmitters.

When you've practiced and are skilled at going into reverie, you can dialogue with your unconscious and ask questions. Wait in the silence for the answers to come back to you. Or, you may initiate visualizations for what you want to see happen.

VISUALIZATIONS

Visualizations represents one element of self-programming. Plan your visualizations, like planning a vacation. If you want to stop drinking or abusing prescription drugs to relax, visualize feeling confident and relaxed in a number of settings. Visualize yourself refusing to take a drink or pills. See yourself sober and abstinent in several scenes. Create images of being socially at ease and confident, with a relaxed personality. Visualize the type of personality you want. Then visualize yourself in a number of situations becoming that type of personality. See yourself being more tolerant of others.

Ask your Higher Self, that spiritual part of yourself, to "mellow out" your personality and heal you. You'll know when to end the relaxation session. End it by saying, "*Do it.*" When you are finished say a prayer of thankfulness and then take some kind of positive action. Start your visualizations while you're in alpha and drift into theta brain wave activity. Don't wait until you're in theta to introduce the visualizations, because that might pull you out of it, unless you've practiced a lot. If your visualization shifts while you're in reverie, go with it. Trust your unconscious.

You're planting seeds in the unconscious with your visualizations. When your visualization starts to move away from you, it's planted like a seed in the fertile soil of your mind. If it doesn't move away from you, it didn't get planted. Once it's planted, *leave it alone*! If you think, "I wonder how long it will take," or "I wonder if it will work," that's like digging up the seed you worked so hard to plant. A farmer doesn't go out into his plowed field, and dig up his seedlings to see how much they've grown. The same is true for visualizations. After you've done a visualization, you may want to repeat it, but otherwise, leave it alone.

HEALING

Relaxation routines need to be done on a daily basis to return your body to a normal state. You can become so skilled at relaxing you will relax when you need or desire to do so. Relaxation induces biochemical and electrical changes in the body that contribute in a positive way to healing.

Personality transformations take place when you heal on these levels. Your appearance may even change—for the better. Your greatest treasure is the healing of your wounds.

CHAPTER 14

PRAYER & MEDITATION

Rubar was born in India and grew up with his parents and eight brothers and sisters. This wealthy family had a meditation chapel in their home for family and friends. Rubar's father realized his children would have little chance to advance in India. He sent his children to different countries for an education and a new life.

PANIC NO MORE

Rubar came to the U.S.A. and earned a Ph.D. in Chemistry. Shortly after graduation he married an American woman and started a family. "Meditation makes you feel peaceful," he said. "I want to make money and have lots of things. I won't care about material things if I meditate." So he stopped. All went well for a while. He bought one home, then another. Soon he owned several rental properties. In India the man makes the decisions for the family. This didn't go well with his liberated wife. After years of struggling with a marriage counselor, Rubar learned to treat his wife with equality, and he stopped trying to arrange marriages for their children.

His wealth continued to grow. He wanted a larger, more expensive home for his family. He picked one that was financially beyond his reach. With help from his wife's family, he managed to get it.

Suddenly, the economy slumped. Houses weren't worth as much. His income from his job was cut. Rubar started having trouble breathing. He gasped for air, his heart raced, and he thought he was dying. He blamed the food, his wife, and the air. He started drinking heavily in the evening.

Rubar could have sold some of his houses at a loss, and removed some of the pressure. But he grasped his possessions all the tighter. He saw his world threatening to collapse. Then he remembered what it was like to meditate and the peace it brought him.

He turned back to the ancient ways of meditation and felt peaceful. His concentration improved. Rubar devised a plan whereby he could keep his property.

He moved his family into one of their rental properties, and rented out the larger house. He learned to live in two worlds at the same time. The inner world of peace and his outer world of materialism.

PRAYER AND MEDITATION

You may be so caught up in your fears of having panic attacks, that you forget you have an inner world. If so, a vague emptiness may permeate your life.

Fear based thoughts and attitudes contribute to panic attacks and limitation, while prayer and meditation create an openness for the source of life.

PRAYER

Prayer and meditation reduce stress, panic and anxiety by acquainting you with your spiritual self. In prayer, you talk to God. You tell the Divine all about yourself, just as you would a trusted friend. Don't hold back. Surrender up your insecurities, fears, anxieties, your anger, depression, disappointments, your hopes and wishes to God.

You build a relationship, as any other relationship, by sharing your whole self. It cannot grow if you share only a mask or small portion of yourself. God accepts all of you, the good, bad and indifferent. From this unconditional acceptance, your experience of love and trust grow. Love is the opposite of fear. Love helps you release some of the negativity and fear that cause panic attacks.

For centuries people conceptualized God as something unobtainable for the ordinary person. God was thought of as some mysterious phantom floating around in the sky in a long white robe. But God is there for you to communicate with. As you go inward through meditation and prayer to the source of life, you have an experience of the Divine within yourself.

The acceptance of a Divine being can be enormously comforting. You learn to trust that there is an added dimension to yourself, something larger than your small, personal world.

Pray to the Divine with confidence and a feeling of closeness, as if you were a small child talking to your mother or father. A half-believing prayer is insufficient. Most people don't get any response because of their disbelief. If you pray and say a little prayer and then start thinking of something else, or pray, "Heavenly Father, I need a new car," or "I'm awfully sleepy now, amen," don't expect much.

If you talk to God with all your heart, and make up your mind, "God will talk to me," and refuse to believe differently, one day that divine power will respond.

Look for answers in dreams or things that stand out to you. An intuition that comes out of nowhere, something a child said, or a sign along the road may be a message from God.

MEDITATION

Meditation is another, deeper path to God. In meditation, you go further into the stillness and quiet and attune your human consciousness with God's will. This creates a partnership and a strength you can draw on in all areas of your life.

The goal of meditation, much like prayer, is to make a spiritual connection with the source of your being. Meditation calms the mind, dissolves negative attitudes, thoughts and feelings.

Meditation allows you to see yourself—and how you created your own world from your illusions, perceptions, beliefs, fears, and habits. Until you are consciously aware of your motives and actions, you may live in disharmony with life. But in the stillness of meditation, you can view your creation of the world with understanding.

Meditation differs from deep relaxation, although deep relaxation is a side effect of meditation. In deep relaxation, you want to see the images that spring up, and later discover their meaning. In meditation, you ignore the images, continually going deeper and deeper into the light to find your source.

In meditation, images are considered happenings of the mind. When you see them, or feel or hear them, there is usually an experience of knowing and understanding what they are about. Do not allow yourself to become distracted by the images. That is not the concern of the meditator. The seeker in meditation seeks the spiritual. So when images arise, they are simply observed and discarded. There is no need to remember or analyze them, because in meditation the light heals when you let them go.

The discipline of meditation strengthens the ego and personality structure. By learning to *let go*, of images of feelings and thoughts that arise during meditation, you learn to discipline the mind. This carries over into all areas of your life. Then, when fearful thoughts arise that contribute to panic attacks, you can say to yourself, *let go*, and return your mind to the task at hand. Meditation helps the structure of the personality reorganize in a more healthful and positive manner.

If you have a garden, you need to cultivate it and pull the weeds so what you grow has greater abundance. Think of your mind as a garden that needs tending. Meditation helps you become more aware of the thoughts you think, giving you greater power and control over them.

BREATH COUNTING

Meditation is hard work. It requires discipline to do it every day. It is even harder work to keep your mind from wandering. One simple meditation technique is to count your breath. You close your eyes and count silently each time you breathe out.

Count "one" for the first breath, "two" for the second breath, "three" for the third breath, "four" for the fourth, and then start over with "one" again. Continue counting for ten minutes. When your mind wanders, gently but firmly pull it back and continue counting.

Breath counting is designed to teach and practice the ability to do one thing at a time. If worked at consistently, it has definite positive psychological and physiological effects.

NON-ATTACHMENT

One of the goals of meditation is to develop an attitude of non-attachment. People are usually attached in varying degrees to their possessions. In fact, some people appear to be owned by their possessions, especially a house or car or symbols of status or security. While a devout meditator appreciates having those possessions, they do not occupy a central core of attachment in the mind.

Attachments keep you stuck on physical levels. A meditator wishes to transcend the physical into the spiritual realms.

Some people hesitate to meditate and release their images and feelings because they think they won't be themselves if they do. This is a false assumption. You are not your images, thoughts or feelings. They are simply energies that either get stuck in you or pass through you.

Visualize an illuminated golden core of light splattered with oil, dirt and mold. You need to wipe it clean to appreciate its full radiance. Meditation allows you to dissolve these negative elements, the energies of fear, anger, greed, egoism, lust, and addictive behaviors. It takes you into a greater awareness of yourself—your *golden core of light*. The divine light is always there. It is a part of you. You cannot lose it.

PATTERNS OF ENERGY

Your life is composed of many habits and patterns of energy. Some good, some not so good. These habits often determine your behavior either consciously or unconsciously. For example, you may be conditioned to think you are your body and nothing more.

You might take an insult about your body to be an insult to you. But if you think of your body like a house you live in, you can be more open and objective. Your house may have some rooms that are sunny and bright. Others may be dark and never used.

Your spirituality is one room. Your mental capacities, physical body and emotions are other rooms.

One room, or aspect of yourself may be over developed and others ignored. For example, you may live largely in your mind while neglecting your physical form. Meditation helps blend your mental, emotional, physical and spiritual aspects in harmony.

The results of meditation are greater efficiency in everyday life and comprehension of a different view of reality than the one you ordinarily use. You become aware of another world, an inner spiritual world. You learn how to, *go home.*

AWARENESS

Meditation, when combined with a program of self-change, leads you to peace of mind. The self-change aspect of meditation involves developing a conscious awareness of your habits, reactions and intentions. Self-honesty is essential to self-change. The goal is to become totally self-aware, no matter how painful, embarrassing, or frustrating it may be.

To help you become more self-aware, go through the following list taken from Audle Allison's handbook, *Meditation*. Work on one aspect of self-awareness each week. Write the aspect down you are working on and take it with you wherever you go. Refer to it frequently and write down your responses. The different self-awareness aspects are designed to build upon one another, so take them in order.

1. I will watch the events of my environment to discover the ideas, objects, and emotions that attract my attention.
2. I will realize what I am most interested in, and the reasons why I am interested.
3. I will watch the way my mind works to support my interest and attention. I will realize if that causes me benefits or problems.
4. I will reassure myself of finding my spiritual connection three times each day.
5. I will watch the way my life is organized. When I have to change my pattern of living, I will notice my reaction.
6. When I find myself in an objectionable situation, I will use the situation to build self control. I will adapt and accept the situation, rather than misdirecting my energies into frustration and hate.
7. When my mind is filled with the kind of thought that I wouldn't want anyone else to know I'm thinking, I will break up the unwanted thought pattern. (A mental scream, or some other abrupt statement will pull the mind away and shatter the pattern.)
8. I will not force anyone to do anything. I will go within and ask for what I want done, mentally sending the *Golden Light of Love* to the person involved. (Close your eyes and picture the face of the person involved, and mentally project golden light around them.)

Be supportive of your awareness' and write them down in your journal. Becoming self-aware will not automatically change you, but it does give you the ability to make corrections. Then take action.

DIVINE POWER

When you meditate, you can eventually tap into your divine power. When that happens, you've got to handle it. Many people automatically assume as soon as that power begins to come into their life, they are changed. That all the old passes away. And in a sense, that's true. But you still have to learn how to deal with the energy, how to use it and how to incorporate it into the fabric of your being.

For instance, if you fall in love, that doesn't automatically give you good sense. There are enormous mistakes made in the name of love. The same is true of connecting with your divine power. So it needs to be taken in steps for you to get used to it. Don't forget your common sense when you're working with higher energies.

MEDITATION GROUPS

In starting your meditation path, it's most helpful to find a meditation group and a teacher or Guru to show you the way. Meditating in a group heightens the power and experience. Other group advantages are that you have someone to talk to about your meditations. Most cities have meditation centers, and offer their services for a donation or small cost. If someone asks you for a large sum of money to instruct you, look elsewhere.

There are numerous kinds and types of meditation techniques. If you are doing a particular meditation and you don't feel it's right for you, stop doing it. Investigate other methods until you find one that is. The following meditation is taken from Audle Allison's handbook, *Meditation*, and taught at the Lotus Centers located in Oklahoma City, and Tulsa, Ok., Dallas and Austin, Texas, and the Mountain Institute at Red River and Taos, N.M.

ENVIRONMENT FOR MEDITATION

It's best to meditate after any food you've eaten has digested. Select a quiet spot, away from distractions. Darken the room to outside light. You might want a picture of your spiritual leader to help you get into the attitude of reverence. A chair or pillow is fine to sit on, but always sit upright. Keep the spine, neck and head in a straight line. This allows energy to flow through the body with the least amount of resistance. If possible, use a blanket or wear the same clothes each time you meditate because they collect energy from your meditations. It's easier to build meditation into a habit if you do it at the same time each day.

FIRST MEDITATION TECHNIQUE

It helps to know and understand what you're doing and why it's done in meditation. The first technique in meditation is called *Running The Light.* It helps you become aware of the etheric energy (also known as the life force) constantly flowing through your physical form from head to toe. The energy is visualized as golden light. Before you can direct this spiritual energy, you must experience it.

To begin meditation, touch the forefinger and thumb of each hand together to form a circle, and place your hands, palms down, on your knees. Sit cross-legged or in the lotus posture on the floor, or cross your legs at the ankles if you're sitting in a chair.

You need to keep your body as still as possible for thirty minutes while you meditate, so get comfortable. It's harder to direct your consciousness if your legs hurt or your back aches. Quiet the mind and still the body. Go into an attitude of surrender to your Higher Self.

Now, close your eyes and focus your attention at the top of your head. By focusing there, you block some of the etheric energy as it enters your body. Visualize the energy as golden light. As the blocked energy builds up, you may feel a pressure, or a slight tingling sensation. Whatever it is, become aware of the energy.

Next, with your mind, mentally direct this energy (golden light) down through your head to the space between your eyebrows, then down your neck, dividing it at the neck and flowing the energy down both arms into the hands and fingers.

When you have moved the energy (golden light) properly there is a warmth, pulsation, or a feeling of fullness in your hands. Go slowly at first. You must consciously feel the energy and see the light moving every step of the way before you can learn to handle it.

After feeling the energy in your hands, leave it there and return your attention to the top of the head. Concentrate again until you're aware of the energy building up. Now, move it again through the head to the space between the eyebrows, also known as the point of will. Then move it down the neck and the spinal cord.

As the energy moves down the spine, you may experience areas of coolness, tingling, heat, and even pain. If so, simply relax and let the energy flow. These blockages will dissolve in time as you flow the light through them.

At the base of the spine, separate the energy and move it down both legs to the knees. Now join the energy you left in your hands with the energy in your knees. You will feel a slight surge as they unite. Now direct all the energy you have built up down both legs and out the soles of your feet into the earth. Be sure to move the energy completely out of the body.

Always offer a brief prayer of thanks to your Higher Self for allowing you to become conscious of the divine energy. Give thanks for what you receive and develop a thankful attitude. That allows you to receive even more.

Return your concentration to the top of the head and do two more rounds of *Running The Light.* During the second round, hold in your mind thoughts of cleansing and healing your body as the energy moves through it. During the third round, be thankful for the peace that has been brought into the body.

SECOND MEDITATION TECHNIQUE

The second technique is called *Listening In And Holding The Light*. To *Listen In*, close your eyes and place your forefingers on the cheekbones at the base of your eyes. Press up slightly on the bottom of your eyes. Roll your eyes upward as much as you can and put your head back. Leaving the forefingers in this position, close each ear with your thumbs by pressing gently on the outer flap at the ear opening.

Listen for the *Om* sound, pronounced *aum*. Use the mantra *Om*, as you breathe out. Search for that sound. You may see patterns of lights. Then move your head back to the normal upright position and take your hands down and look into the light.

When you *Listen In* the first time, you may see images of geometrical patterns of light, perhaps a golden circle, or two crescent moons facing one another or a star off in the distance. The color you see indicates your level of consciousness.

The golden light represents the Christ level of consciousness. The lesson taught on this level is compassion. If you see a red color, clap your hands and that will cause you to go into the next higher vibrational level.

Then, listen in for a second and a third time. The second time you listen in, you might see a blue color. The blue represents the cosmic mind, the *All Seeing All Knowing Eye,* which is described in the Bible and also depicted on the one dollar bill. This is the level of consciousness from which knowledge from the universe is gained. It also brings a profound feeling of peace.

On the third viewing strive to see reflections of the *white light, brighter than ten thousand suns.* The light is your protector and you are to move with it into the Self. The *Om* sound is your guide to take you home. What you see is only a reflection and shadow of the true reality. When you can move through the light, past the *Om* sound into the stillness, you are in your spiritual home.

THIRD MEDITATION TECHNIQUE

The third meditation technique involves going into the stillness. Focus your attention at the top of your head. Imagine you are surrounded by light. The light protects you. Chant *Om* silently as you breathe out. The vibration from the mantra *Om* breaks up negative thought and energy patterns, freeing you from their effects.

Observe whatever comes into your mind. Do not act or think about it. Become the watcher of the mind as it moves into its desires. Do not resist the flow of thoughts in your consciousness, but watch them drift by like clouds. A thought or feeling may surface and get stronger. Continue to chant *Om* on the out breath. A thought or image may suddenly disappear and a part of your body may jerk, particularly at the neck or back. This will not hurt you. Then all memory of what you were thinking or feeling is dissolved like it was never there. Continue with your mantra and meditation. Jerry Densow, Director of the Mountain Institute, refers to this as, *God calling you home.*

When you first begin the process of meditation, the mind is active and full of images and ideas. Thoughts come into your consciousness begging for attention. Your mind may even create distractions to avoid the discipline. In time you will perceive the subtle sounds and lights and move to the source of your being. Meditation is a lifelong pursuit. Change occurs slowly, over a long time.

When you focus your mind on one thing, it becomes quiet. Concentration harmonizes your mental, physical, emotional, and spiritual bodies. There are many techniques that do this. One is to repeat a mantra or chant, over and over. *Om*, pronounced *aum*, is the Sanskrit sound for the energy of the universe. Sanskrit is the first language known to exist on earth. *Om* is the mantra commonly used by meditation students. As you go deep into meditation and become one with it, you actually hear the *Om* sound.

FOURTH MEDITATION TECHNIQUE

Another technique to use along with the mantra, *Om*, is to look at the flame of a candle, then close your eyes and continue to visualize the flame. Move into the light and imagine that you are a tiny image sitting on top of your head in the light. Become one with it.

Metaphorically, the flame distills and burns the impurities from you while you meditate. Keep returning your mind to the mantra and the light as thoughts and images arise.

Contemplation of one thought, such as love, or the power of God, can build concentration. Or, you can look at the space between your eyebrows, your spiritual eye. Still another technique is to picture the face of a spiritual teacher in your mind. Imagine the light of your spiritual teacher's eyes flowing to you.

When other thoughts arise, simply realize you have strayed from your goal of meditation. Gently return your attention to the mantra and what you are to concentrate on. Beware of the sensations, or other phenomenon that might distract you from your goal in meditation. If you let yourself get sidetracked, you will not progress.

WHAT YOU CONCENTRATE ON, YOU BECOME

As you develop concentration, you learn that what you concentrate upon, you become. Concentrate only on that which is positive and life affirming. Concentrating upon fear makes you fearful. Concentrating upon anger or hate makes you angry or hateful. Concentrating upon God produces a Godlike consciousness. Ask, *Father, may I become one with you? How may I serve you?*

Meditate as long as you feel comfortable, but try for at least thirty minutes daily. When images or perceptions arise, bless them and let them go. Always strive to go further into the light. Before you stop meditating, picture the face of a loved one and surround them in love and light. When you desire to come out of meditation, picture your own face in front of you, rub your eyes and open them.

Meditating will help you grow and develop as a total human being. You will find long-lost parts of yourself. Your capacity to cope, love and relate to others and express your feelings will increase and deepen. You will begin to know that each of us is a part of all others and that you are never alone. Walk in light and live in peace.

CHAPTER 15

CREATIVE VISUALIZATIONS & AFFIRMATIONS

Visualizations offer you the possibility of directing your life by using higher energies. They are stepping stones out of your personal mire. Like tiny seeds you plant in the soil of the subconscious mind, with care and nurturing, visualizations grow and blossom into new realities.

A visualization is a simple process. Close your eyes, relax and imagine in your mind the way you want to be. It is important to feel as though you are already in the situation when you visualize. See it in the present. Use as many internal senses as possible. See the smile on your face. Hear the sound of your voice. Feel yourself being confident and secure. What is important is the feeling and energy behind the visualization. Believe in your mind that it is so. Visualizations can be short and consist of several seconds, or they can last as long as several hours.

A visualization can consist of nothing more than seeing yourself shopping and picking out something you like with ease and confidence.

Design your visualization in advance. Decide what you want to create and set a goal of when you want to achieve it. How many days, weeks, or months do you think it will take? Be realistic. Visualizations take time to build up energy in the unconscious. The things you wish to change may be the result of conditioning or mental habits. Three weeks of consistent effort using visualizations is the average time it takes to change a habit.

If you want to go into a social situation and feel comfortable and relaxed, visualize every step of the way. Construct a mental scene in your mind of whatever you wish to achieve in vivid detail. Visualize the color of your clothes, the dust on your shoes, smells, and how you want to feel. Then allow your unconscious to process the new changes you want to make.

AFFIRMATIONS

Use the power of affirmations to further enhance your visualizations. An affirmation means to *make firm*. State it in the positive as though it has already come into being. For instance, when doing visualizations for confidence in social situations, state, "I am confident, peaceful and serene in social situations." Repeat your affirmations throughout the day. When you're driving the car, doing housework, or exercising—not just while you're relaxed.

The following affirmations have worked well for many people.

- Peace and serenity flow into my life.
- I am whole, strong, and healthy.
- Peace, be still.
- Whatever needs to be revealed to me will be.
- Nothing can keep me from my good.
- The truth has the ability to reveal itself.
- I am confident and full of enthusiasm.
- The past is gone and I am totally open to the new.

The best affirmations are ones you make up yourself, because they fit your individual needs. They are usually best when kept short. Use words that are intense and magnetic, words that feel and mean a lot to you. Affirmations can be spoken out loud, written, or said internally to yourself. Always state them with positive energy, in the present tense, as though they already exist. The more you use them, the easier and more effective they become.

Do not create affirmations like, "I now feel less fearful." The focus on negative energy is likely to produce conflict. The energy of the new will push out the old. Conflicts are never resolved on the same level they are created. You mature out of the conflict.

The more energy you put into your visualizations and affirmations, the faster they work. If you don't see the images you construct, that's fine. Simply imagine what you want.

PROGRAMMING NEW BEHAVIOR

Visualizations usually need to be done daily for twenty-one days when programming for new behaviors. In addition, repeat your affirmations ten times a day for the twenty-one days. Set attainable goals. If you're working through a deep-seated negative habit pattern, you may need to continue your visualizations and affirmations longer.

OVERCOMING BLOCKS

If you feel blocked, you may have a negative energy pattern that actively prevents your success. Although there are many exercises to overcome blocks, I will give two of my favorites. The first is an easy technique to help you locate and overcome blocks.

Get two pieces of paper and a pen. Go into a relaxed state. Now write the goal you are to achieve on the first piece of paper. Then put down all the reasons you can't. Be honest. When you're finished, read through them. Feel how useless these reasons are. Rip up the piece of paper and throw it away. Feel the negative chains that bind you break apart.

Now on the other piece of paper write down all your positive intentions and feelings about the change you want to bring into being. Take some time to finish. You can also add positive affirmations such as:

- I am totally open to this goal.
- Positivity guides me to attaining my desire.

Repeat the blockbuster exercise as often as you need to. Negative patterns are also stopped by changing the way you relate in the present—through sorting out negativity and focusing on the positive.

The second exercise to overcome blocks is a visualization. In a relaxed state, imagine you are walking down a path. Suddenly you come upon a boulder blocking the path. Push the boulder aside. If it is too large, pick up a stick and beat it until it breaks down and you can move it. You can also imagine a friend or teacher helping you.

When the boulder is pushed aside, notice the ground under where it had been. If it's solid, then continue down the path. But if there is a hole or cavern underneath, explore it and find out what's in it. Caverns can indicate some abuse or trauma has taken place. You may find your wounded child. If so, then do the inner child exercise found in Chapter 19.

Sometimes, you may not see anything, but a feeling will appear. Perhaps fear, perhaps anger. Allow the full feeling to develop. Or you may hear a tiny voice inside your head talking. Do not respond, but simply allow it to be. As the energy arises, it will evaporate and remove the block. If something happens you need to process, consult a psychotherapist.

Sandra, a thirty-year old woman, had suffered from irritable bowel syndrome for fifteen years. She had taken a variety of prescribed medications continuously for several years, and was "an authority on Freudian psychodynamics," but had no relief. She could not go more than one hundred feet from a bathroom and was becoming suicidal over the fact that she could hardly leave her home. She was instructed to use the following affirmations while placing the palms of her hands over her abdomen.

- The healing powers of my body are healing this area.
- My abdomen is calm, quiet, and peaceful.
- Warmth and quietness are spreading throughout the whole lower section of my body.

- My entire GI tract does its work smoothly and quietly with no unnecessary activity.

In addition, Sandra was shown a picture of a normal GI tract. She visualized the first time what she thought her GI tract looked like, then switched to visualizing the picture of a normal GI tract.

Sandra's emotional upsets and her body came under control over the next five months. She was able to stop taking all medication and lead a normal life. She "became a new person" using visualizations and affirmations.

SENSORY SYSTEMS

Visualizations encompass all the sensory systems, not just visual. Hearing sounds or having feelings or smells can also be termed visualizations.

Learning specialists classify the population into hearing or auditory learners, visual learners, and feeling learners.

- Visual learners base their decisions on what something looks like to them.
- Hearing learners (auditory) base their decisions on facts, data, and information.
- Feeling learners (kinesthetic) base their decisions on how something makes them feel.

Everyone has one dominate system they use to make decisions. The other systems are used as secondary systems, and some may be deleted altogether.

VISUAL LEARNERS

When visual learners relax and close their eyes, they go into alpha brain wave consciousness, and switch to another system—

to feeling or hearing. So if you're a "visual person," don't expect to see much internally, because your secondary sensory system is either "feeling" or "hearing." However, you can train yourself to see visually.

HEARING LEARNERS

If you're a hearing learner (auditory), then your secondary sensory system in alpha brain wave consciousness is either visual or feelings. Whatever it is, use that secondary system to reprogram yourself. Or, practice seeing visualizations until your mind learns how to produce them.

FEELING LEARNERS

If you're a feeling learner (kinesthetic), create what feelings you want while doing a new behavior. Put in sounds and what you feel things look like, too. Make it as real as possible so your visualization sends the message to reprogram your subconscious mind and manifest what you want.

MANIFESTING NEW BEHAVIORS

Your subconscious mind doesn't know the difference between the outer reality and a visualization. Visualizations are practice sessions for your mind. When you visualize a new behavior it becomes familiar to you. Then, when you go into an actual situation, the new behavior feels like second nature.

Visualizations done consistently on a daily basis following meditation can have powerful results in overcoming fears and anxieties. During meditation, you're doing mental house cleaning. You're letting go of rigid or frozen patterns of thinking and negative energy. And you're creating a vacuum.

If you take a behavior away, replace it with a positive one. If you don't release or correct the negative energy that produced the undesired behavior, it may erupt into another behavior equally as bad. Be what you are as a result of intention, and not by accident.

Visualization is the language of the subconscious mind. That's why you tell your mind what you want by using visualizations. That fills the vacuum. Otherwise, the vacuum may be filled at random by your subconscious with things you'd rather not do. When you use meditations, visualizations and affirmations, you manifest your own reality using spiritual energy. You take control of your life.

When you include visualizations as part of your meditations, you contact a higher energy source to work through. If you do twenty per cent of the work, your Higher Self does the other eighty per cent. When you approach change in this manner, what you do can be effective. When change comes, be ready to accept it with open arms. Be supportive of the new ways that emerge. Nurture them as you would a very young baby. In time, the positive new ways of being will replace the old personality structure of fear and intimidation.

Visualizations usually take time to develop into reality. But they can also take the first time you do them. The more skilled you are, the quicker your mind can seize the idea and put it to work for you.

One client practiced visualizing herself confident in social situations for several hours before going to a party. She was surprised she could feel so comfortable, at ease and socially poised. In fact, she experienced an enjoyment of being with others she had never felt before. Later, when she recounted her experience with me, she said, "I didn't feel like myself at all. I wasn't even afraid. There wasn't even a wall around me. It was wonderful."

Even when visualizations work this well, don't stop visualizing. It's possible to effect a sudden change from all the positive energy you pour into it, only to have it dry up and leave you as before when you stop putting energy into it.

Your behavior is composed of habits that are deeply grooved into your personality structure. To change your behavior, and the way you think and feel, you must constantly support and nurture yourself. Reward yourself by doing special things when you feel a positive shift in your behavior. Thank yourself for caring enough to do the hard work that makes the change possible.

TRAINING THE MIND TO VISUALIZE

If you have difficulty imaging, simple practice exercises can help. Look at a picture. Explore the subject in depth. Notice the detail, the colors, and the shapes and sizes of the images. Then close your eyes and recall the picture.

When you open your eyes, look at the picture again, and observe how much you recalled. Then examine the picture again, close your eyes and remember what it looked like. Open your eyes and make the comparison. Continue to do this with several objects.

This kind of practice trains your mind to remember. Visualize and sharpen your awareness of surroundings. Visualize what your car looks like, what a new hair style would look like on you, or rearrange the furniture in your home. The more you practice, the easier it gets.

If you find a blank wall staring at you when you visualize, you may be blocked in that sensory system. To test for a blockage, simply hold your head still and turn your eyes upward to your right. If this position hurts, or is impossible to put your eyes in, you're probably blocked in your imagination and creativity.

This frequently happens if you were reared by someone who was over controlling and didn't allow you to learn how to do things on your own. The way to unlock your creativity is to continue looking up to the right with your eyes ever so often until it feels comfortable.

Creative visualizations can be fun and rewarding. Make a list of behaviors you want to change. If you feel uncomfortable in certain situations, do visualizations seeing yourself relaxed and confident in them. Make your visualizations real in every way. See the colors in your clothes, smell the odors in the air, feel the furniture. The more energy you put into it, the faster your visualization works.

After you can visualize easily, you don't always need a deep state of relaxation to do it. You can visualize with your eyes open. Be wildly creative in your visualizations. You can create visualizations for new behaviors, release negative energy and program yourself to get a better and higher paying job.

BREAKING NEGATIVE ATTACHMENTS

Ending a relationship that's gone sour or is stifling using visualizations can heal the pain faster. Visualize yourself and the other person in the relationship and see a cord attaching the two of you. Then mentally burn the cord, say good-bye and walk away. Visualizations can help resolve conflicts with those persons who have died in your life. See yourself with the deceased. Tell him or her what you feel and think. Have the image respond back to you. Continue doing the visualization until you feel all the energy has gone out of the relationship and you can let it go.

Visualizations are different from daydreams. In daydreams you just wish. But you approach visualizations with a conviction that they work. You put consistent energy into them, and then reap the rewards.

BE CREATIVE

Your subconscious loves variety and novelty. The more creative and artistic you are, the higher evolved your results. Using the language of metaphors and symbolism, you can reach areas of your being not touched by words. You may want to play soft music to help deepen your visualizations.

The following is a guided visualization for reclaiming your inner child. *Image yourself walking in the country, coming upon a lake, and jumping into it. You swim to the bottom where you find a trap door, which you go through. There you see winding stairs that go down and around until you finally reach the bottom. Then you realize you're in a dungeon filled with cobwebs.*

Suddenly you notice a young child that is your younger self chained to the dungeon wall. You find a saw and free your younger self. Then the two of you run to escape the dungeon. But the cobwebs grab and hold the two of you back. You look up and see names on the cobwebs. Perhaps your mother or an uncle or some other name appears. You tear them away from you and your younger self. Then you find a hole in the wall and escape.

But outside there are dragons and other monsters. An angel comes and gives you a magic cape of protection. You put on the magic cape, and holding your younger self, run to freedom.

You are only limited by your imagination in creating visualizations. Color is a useful tool in letting go of accumulated negative energy. For instance, you can imagine red to symbolize anger. The old saying, "She was so mad she saw red," may be true. To release anger, see yourself blowing your red breath into pink balloons. Tie a knot in them, and see them float away from you.

Ask yourself what color the energy of fear represents to you. If it's black, that may mean what you fear is actually from the past and is dead energy. If it's dark and murky green, it might symbolize some kind of threat to your security. If it's red, it might mean you're afraid of your own rage or anger. Whatever color it is, ask your Higher Self what that color means to you.

You can also release fear using the balloon method, or simply visualize the color of the fear energy draining from your body into the ground as you do the *Running The Light* meditation exercise described in Chapter 14. Follow up with an affirmation, "I now accept positive energy flowing into me."

Ask the fear what it's doing for you. Usually the answer is, "I'm trying to protect you." If so, ask your creative side to find better ways to protect you instead of making you fearful. You may get an image of yourself doing something different.

Once you get the idea what the feeling or energy of anger or fear is doing for you, design a visualization using positive energy to replace it.

If you have a tendency to see others as stronger than you are, notice to whom you project your energy. A centering visualization is to close your eyes and imagine scattered energy all around you, like tiny lights in the darkness. Pretend there is a giant magnet inside you, pulling the fragmented lights back to you. When you open your eyes, you'll probably be surprised at the difference.

HEALING VISUALIZATIONS

Visualizations can help heal splitting and fragmentation in the personality (mood swings and seeing someone or something as all good or all bad are examples of splitting and fragmentation that often leads to panic attacks).

The two hands visualization method of visualization requires your eyes open. Hold out both palms of your hands. Visualize yourself in a negative mood in one hand, and put a color on it. Then in the other hand, see yourself in a positive mood, and put a color on it.

Pick out two moods of equal intensity in energy. If you pick out a negative feeling that's much stronger than your positive one, you may wipe out the positive one. You can increase your positive feelings by combining several positive visualizations. When the negative and positive visualizations are equal, or the positive visualizations stronger, your mind will integrate them easier. Mix the colors together, and very slowly put your hands together. Then hold the palms of your hands over your heart. What color did you end up with?

If you divide people into "all good" and "all bad" types, you might visualize a person's good traits in one hand and imagine a color on that hand. Then visualize the same person with his or her bad traits in the other hand, and imagine a color on that hand. Blend the colors. State a positive affirmation, "Everyone is a combination of both positive and negative traits." You can also visualize the "good" and "bad" parts of yourself using the same process. This will help you feel more integrated.

A complaint I've heard many times when clients do this is, "The colors don't want to be together," or, "I don't want that to be a part of my personality." The purpose of this visualization is to integrate the different aspects of your personality. You may need to have the two parts of yourself talk to each other until they agree to merge. When you can fold your hands together, hold them over your heart. This integrates the different aspects of yourself into your emotional center, your heart.

You can program yourself with visualizations and affirmations for almost anything. They can be used for self-healing, selling property, or finding a suitable relationship as well as changing ingrained personality traits. These types of visualizations can be done less frequently than those programming new behaviors. Simply visualize what you want and affirm it. It's very important to believe in what you're doing. If you do a visualization, and then think, well, that won't happen, you cancel out the good effects of your visualization. Once you do a visualization, keep the thought constant in your mind that it is so. If doubts creep in, quickly refocus your mind with a positive affirmation. Visualizations and affirmations will enhance your effectiveness and ability to change. They are commitments for a better life.

CHAPTER 16

ASSERTIVENESS

A friend asks to borrow your new, expensive camera . . . Someone cuts in front of you in line . . . A salesperson is annoyingly persistent . . . .

For panic attack victims, these examples represent anxious, stressful situations because they are often conditioned to be passive and please others. They allow others to impose on them because they feel their rights don't count. Besides their learned helplessness, many panic attack victims frequently apologize and use non-assertive language such as:

- may be
- just
- only
- there's no problem
- I wonder if you could
- I can't
- it's not important
- you know
- I mean
- I guess
- well
- don't bother

Non-assertive body posture reflects downcast eyes, the shifting of weight, a slumped body, the wringing of hands, or a whining, hesitant, or giggly tone of voice that says, "Don't take me seriously." A person with a passive communication style avoids conflicts, tension and confrontation. The result is that you don't get your needs met.

These characteristics often make panic attack victims vulnerable for exploitation by aggressive, controlling or manipulative individuals. One panic attack victim exclaimed she had bought over one hundred dollars of magazine subscriptions from a salesman who had knocked on her door. She didn't want to hurt the salesman's feelings by saying "No," even though buying the subscriptions meant she wouldn't be able to pay her rent.

NON-ASSERTIVE PHILOSOPHY

If you have trouble saying "No," a non-assertive philosophy may hinder you from taking control of your life. Consider the following ideas. If you believe they are true, you probably have difficulty being assertive.

ASSERTIVENESS

1. Others have the right to judge my thoughts, feelings, and actions.
2. I must always have a reason, excuse, or justification for my thoughts, feelings, and actions.
3. Everything I do must make sense.
4. I must always be logical, rational, and reasonable.
5. I must always be consistent and never change my mind.
6. I must never make mistakes or admit making mistakes.
7. I do not deserve to be treated with respect, especially when I have made a mistake. I should feel guilty.
8. I must know everything, always have an answer, and answer every question. I must never appear ignorant, stupid, or uninformed.
9. I am responsible for finding solutions to other peoples problems.
10. I must always be grateful for and dependent upon the goodwill of others. When others are kind to me, I must do as they wish.
11. I must always understand everything, or act as if I do.
12. I must always care about everything and everybody.
13. Everyone I meet must like me and approve of what I do. If I'm not approved of, it's awful.
14. I am responsible for and have control over other people's feelings.
15. I am responsible for and have control over the consequences of other people's actions.
16. I am not entitled to my own feelings.
17. I must always conform to the expectations of others.
18. People who love me will always approve of my actions.
19. People who don't approve of my actions don't love me.
20. Love and anger are opposites. They are incompatible.

Behavior that stems from these beliefs is often referred to as *milk toast behavior* because these beliefs cause you to be shy and quiet. You acquiesce to others because of your fear of rejection. You are easily exploited, used, and often are a victim of sexual molestation and child abuse. To those who adhere to a non-assertive philosophy, a "victim" pattern develops early in life that is difficult to stop. Once victimized, traumatic situations occur over and over again until the cycle is broken.

But being passive isn't the only communication problem panic attack victims may suffer. Because panic attack victims are usually trying to compensate in one way or another for their fears and anxieties, they may vacillate between being passive aggressive, controlling or manipulative and at times even aggressive.

FOUR TYPES OF COMMUNICATORS

There are four different ways people connect, relate and communicate with one another—*passive, passive-aggressive / manipulative, aggressive, and assertive.* Each style of communication has distinct features associated with body language, beliefs about the world, and the use of language.

PASSIVE-AGGRESSIVE BEHAVIOR

In passive-aggressive behavior, you simply agree to do whatever the other person wants you to do. But then you procrastinate and never do it, or do it wrong. Most teenagers cycle through this phase as they mature. People who adopt a passive-aggressive communication style are often sarcastic, angry, and indirect. Alcoholics often use this style. They hold in their anger and submit to others until they can't stand it any longer, then overreact.

MANIPULATIVE BEHAVIOR

A manipulative communication style is an offshoot of passive-aggressive behavior. It is the type of behavior that is associated with a "con artist."

A manipulative style involves becoming a mirror image of whatever the person you're trying to manipulate wants to think you are. You say what they want to hear. Your body language may be anything—but it reflects what you think others want to see. The goal is to get what you want, often without regard for the other person.

But panic attack victims may also use the manipulative style because they think that's safer. If you've grown up in a home where violence occurred, you quickly learn to agree with others. You tell them what they want to hear in order to avoid further abuse. Also, if you've grown up in a home with manipulative parents, you don't know any better. The feeling behind a manipulative communication style is that you don't have a power of your own.

Women who are taught men are superior, and husbands should be the head of the house often develop a manipulative communication style. They think that's the only way to get their needs met. But the person who is willing to take care of another person, emotionally, physically and financially usually has their own agenda in mind. Your dependency victimizes you and makes you vulnerable to the whims of the other person.

Manipulation and dependency are poor substitutes for a healthy relationship. Often the partners feel cheated because the relationship does not feel "real." They feel emotionally abandoned because no one's really "there" for them. This problem is the core of "relationship addictions." Those caught up in addictive relationships may eventually want to leave the relationship, but don't because they feel too weak.

AGGRESSIVE BEHAVIOR

An aggressive communication style involves using power and intimidation to get control. A threatening body posture may be assumed, such as a puffed out chest, glaring eyes, pointing a finger in an accusing manner, or having the hands on the hips. The body is stiff and rigid, with the feet firmly planted. Aggressive people are rude, loud and overbearing. They may snicker and use a haughty tone of voice to blame and bully people to get their way. They think nothing of walking on others.

The thinking behind this facade comes from an abused background. "No one met my needs. Therefore, I have the right to take what I want to meet my needs." Aggressive people have contempt for those they intimidate. They are known as "steam rollers" and "machine gun" communicators.

Aggressive words include threats, such as "you'd better," "if you don't watch out," put downs, such as "come on," "you must be kidding," evaluative comments such as "should," "bad," and sexist or racist terms.

Aggressive people tend to be dominating, angry and vengeful. They hurt other people's feelings, and don't care. Out of fear people may give aggressive types what they want, but later sabotage them behind their backs. Aggressive types inspire others toward retaliation, resentment, revenge, recrimination and rebellion. Few people like aggressive individuals or trust them with their inner selves.

ASSERTIVE BEHAVIOR

The one communication style panic attack victims usually don't use until they have had counseling, is assertiveness—open, honest and direct communication.

Assertive behavior is the act of standing up for your basic human rights without violating the basic human rights of others.

ASSERTIVENESS

Becoming assertive involves adopting a set of beliefs based on your basic human rights.

Assertion stops the fear and feelings of helplessness and adds the needed control to assume a positive living style. When being assertive, establish good eye contact, stand comfortably but firmly on two feet with your hands loosely at your sides and talk in a low, strong, steady tone of voice.

A high pitched voice is associated with feelings of helplessness. Experiment by talking in a slow, low, tone and then in a high pitched voice, to determine the difference those effects have on you. And it influences others as well—positively or negatively, depending on the pitch, tone, and tempo of your voice.

The following assertiveness questionnaire will help you to determine how assertive you are, and the areas you may need to work on.

ASSERTIVENESS BEHAVIOR QUESTIONNAIRE

Circle the number that best describes you.

1 -never 2 -rarely 3 -sometimes 4 -usually 5 -always

1. I can make my own decisions.		1 2 3 4 5
2. I am myself around prestigious people.		1 2 3 4 5
3. I am comfortable around strangers.		1 2 3 4 5
4. I can express these emotions:	anger	1 2 3 4 5
	happiness	1 2 3 4 5
	affection	1 2 3 4 5
	loss	1 2 3 4 5
5. I am friendly/considerate toward others.		1 2 3 4 5
6. I can accept compliments.		1 2 3 4 5
7. I admit my mistakes.		1 2 3 4 5

8.	When I need help, I ask for it.	1 2 3 4 5
9.	When I'm at fault, I apologize.	1 2 3 4 5
10.	When confused, I ask for clarification.	1 2 3 4 5
11.	When people annoy me, I tell them.	1 2 3 4 5
12.	When treated unfairly, I am assertive.	1 2 3 4 5
13.	I maintain eye contact when talking.	1 2 3 4 5
14.	When someone criticizes me, I listen without becoming defensive.	1 2 3 4 5
15.	I think of myself as O.K.	1 2 3 4 5
16.	I speak up in group situations.	1 2 3 4 5
17.	I talk easily with the opposite sex.	1 2 3 4 5
18.	If I disagree with someone's point of view, I express my opinion.	1 2 3 4 5

Check back over your answers. For the items you marked "1" or "2," ask yourself if these are areas in your behavior that you would like to change. Ask yourself, "What do I gain from staying non-assertive?" "Do I get protection from others?" "Praise for conforming to others' expectations?" "Am I simply maintaining a familiar behavior pattern?"

When you weigh the gains of being assertive (self-esteem, independence, honesty) against the losses of being non-assertive (inability to make decisions, stress, powerlessness), the hard work it takes to change is worth it.

If you have difficulty being assertive, you may not know what your rights are. You may allow others to run over and victimize you. Being passive and avoiding conflict is a conditioned survival strategy.

A study of adult children of alcoholics showed that none of them could assert themselves until they were over twenty, had left their parents' home and had taken either an assertiveness training course or had some counseling.

ASSERTIVENESS

BASIC HUMAN RIGHTS

The ways you find to feel safe as a child becomes the neurosis of your adulthood. In order to free yourself from the prison of your past, it's important to know and firmly accept your rights as a human being.

Your basic human rights include:

1. The right to stand up for yourself.
2. To be treated with respect.
3. To be listened to and taken seriously.
4. To ask for help.
5. To say, "I don't know." "I don't understand."
6. To make mistakes and be responsible for them.
7. To not justify your behavior.
8. To have and express feelings, such as anger.
9. To have and state your own opinions.
10. To question or challenge others.
11. To say "No" without feeling guilty.
12. To be paid fairly for your work.
13. Not to be liked all the time by everybody.
14. To do things of which others may not approve.
15. To set your own priorities.
16. To have the right to feel good about yourself.

While changing your basic attitudes, listen to the way you talk. Make "I" statements such as, "I think," "I want," "I feel," rather than "you know," "you make me feel," or "you make me angry." A true "I" statement says something about how you feel or what you think, without criticizing or blaming the other person and without holding the other person responsible for your feelings or reactions. Watch out for disguised "you" statements like, "I think you are controlling."

When you make assertions, avoid blaming, interpreting, diagnosing, labeling, preaching and putting the other person down. True assertiveness always respects the rights and human dignity of others.

By being assertive, you take responsibility for your own thoughts, feelings, and actions. Other people don't "make" you do or feel anything. You make your own choices based on your own decisions. Others may not agree with what you say (that is their right) but they will respect you. You will also increase your self respect.

Role playing is an important exercise when learning how to be assertive. Ask a friend to rehearse a scene with you before you do a "live" assertion. During your role play, be specific about what you want and need. Do not assume the other person already knows.

Expressing anger is difficult even for experts. Here are some fair fighting rules to follow.

1. Stay in the present; within the last forty-eight hours. Don't go back days or years and drag up old problems.
2. Avoid lecturing and finger pointing.
3. Avoid judging and labeling. ("You're bad") Stay with "I" messages.
4. Avoid blaming. ("It's all your fault.")
5. Use active listening. Repeat to the other person what you heard them say. "What I heard you say is _____."
6. State your message directly. "I am angry about ______."
7. Do not try to make someone "wrong" so you can be "right."
8. Fight about one thing at a time.
9. After your express your anger, release it.

ADAPT AN ASSERTIVE LIFE-STYLE

You may not always get what you want by being assertive, but your chances are greatly improved. You feel better about yourself when you are assertive and the other person knows your position. Assert yourself to say whatever is on your mind—even when you know the other person is not receptive to your message.

As an assertive person, you can express your personal likes and interests spontaneously, rather than stating things in neutral terms. You can say, "I like this person," rather than "he is a good person."

You may speak up for your rights. Do not let others take advantage of you. Say "No" without feeling guilty. It is your right. If you can't say "No," you can't really say "Yes" whole heartedly. This is especially true in sexuality. People who can't say "No" are rarely orgasmic. People who can say "No" and have sex only when they want, are usually orgasmic.

If someone continues to request that you do something you don't want to do, use the broken record routine. For example, if Sally keeps asking to borrow your camera and you don't want to lend it, say "I hear what you're saying, but my answer is no," or, "My answer is no, please do not ask me again," or, "No, I don't want to." Repeat these remarks each time the request is made. You do not have to explain your position. A simple "No" is all that's required. By stating your position clearly and firmly, you eliminate arguments and having to justify yourself.

You can set limits and boundaries with others when they infringe upon your basic rights. For instance, if someone is continually late or misses appointments with you, you can set limits by saying, "I am happy to meet with you, but I feel you've been taking advantage of me. If you continue to disregard me, I won't meet with you again."

Be specific when you make an assertion. Don't make vague requests such as, "I want you to be more sensitive to my needs." Let the other person know specifically what you want, such as, "The best way you can help me is simply to listen. I really don't want advice at this time." Be sure and let others know how you feel and what you are thinking. No one can read your mind.

An assertion may involve describing your feelings and the behavior or the situation that bothers you. Specify what you want and ask for an agreement. Then outline the consequences of keeping the agreement or not keeping it. State, "I feel _____ when___________. I would like _________. If you do this, I will _________.

When making an assertion, be sure what you say agrees with your body language. To say one thing assertively, and have a body posture of a *milk toast* is not convincing. Once you state the consequences, be firm about them. Do not threaten to do things you know won't happen. One woman continually threatened to divorce her husband if he didn't stop drinking. She did nothing to back up her threats, so he ignored what she said.

Think through the effects of the limits you set and be sure you are willing to carry through. Don't expect change to come from hit and run confrontations. Change occurs slowly in close relationships. If you make even a small assertion, you'll get tested many times to see if you *really mean it*.

Don't dismiss an issue by thinking, "It really didn't matter," or "I won't say anything this time." Nothing can kill a relationship faster than letting negativity build up. By the time you do get around to saying something, you're probably so angry you scream, or, have a panic attack.

Counselors refer to "letting things slide" as the *threshold syndrome*. Imagine you're in a room with a person with whom you have a relationship. Each time you let something slide and don't express your feelings, you take a step toward the door. When you arrive at the "threshold," you are out of the relationship.

Most first divorces occur because the partners don't know how to solve problems or discuss issues. When they get to the "threshold," they get a divorce. First marriage partners are usually better suited for each other than subsequent marriage partners. But people often try harder in their second marriage, and that makes it better.

When you handle sensitive issues as they arise, your relationships improve. Letting the other person know how you're feeling, and what you're thinking, can deepen the relationship and strengthen the connection.

Being assertive communicates respect for the other person. It is an honest, direct type of behavior, and an appropriate expression of your feelings, beliefs, and opinions. When you are assertive, others respect you and know where they stand with you. You feel better because you have expressed yourself.

CHAPTER 17

NUTRITION & HERBS

Joy slowly sipped her expresso coffee. She wanted to savor every drop of it. She gazed out the window of the quaint cafe. Suddenly she felt her hands shaking. Her heartbeat fluttered and a panicky feeling took over.

Joy was no stranger to panic attacks. She felt one coming on now. She had learned to watch her thoughts, shift her breathing to her abdomen and to not get upset if she had one. She knew there was no psychological reason for her to have a panic attack at this time. Then she looked at her coffee suspiciously. It was made with double rich coffee and chocolate and steamed milk. She loved the flavor—but not the effects.

CAFFEINE

"Oh, no," she thought sadly. "It's really true that caffeine can cause a panic attack in a person predisposed to having panic attacks. That makes coffee, chocolate, cola drinks, in fact, anything with caffeine in it taboo."

Research has documented that daily heavy caffeine use can cause chronic anxiety in a person with a sensitive system, and panic attacks if a large amount of caffeine is consumed at one time.

COCAINE

Cocaine is derived from the coca tree, just as caffeine is. It should be avoided because it is illegal and because of its negative effects on panic attack victims. Marijuana is another illegal drug that can cause severe panic attacks.

SUGAR

Joy also learned to avoid sugar. From the sugar highs and lows (caused by the elevation and fall in blood sugar,) Joy knew a piece of cake caused her trouble. She experienced the jitters, an inability to concentrate, and depression. Sometimes she ate cake anyway, and then couldn't function for three to fours hours. She would go into a depression, become drowsy, and go to sleep.

GROUNDING FOODS

Joy learned not only what to avoid eating, but what affected her in a positive manner. Because of her high-strung sensitivity,

Joy ate what she called, *grounding foods*. These included potatoes, carrots, and beets. She coined the phrase, *grounding foods,* because she realized that, for her, tubular vegetables that grew in the earth, caused her to feel and concentrate better. Complex carbohydrates from pasta, and whole foods such as rice or barley, when combined with relaxation, help restore the serotonin neurotransmitters damaged by stress, anxiety and panic attacks.

FRUITS

Joy loved fruits. But, if she ate a lot of fruit during the course of a day, she discovered that she would feel a little, "spacy." She liked to eat an apple or banana at breakfast. She found that if she skipped breakfast, later during the day, about three or four o'clock in the afternoon, she usually had a slump. When she ate breakfast the slump didn't happen.

VEGETABLES

Joy knew from reading about nutrition that half of her daily diet should be vegetables. Not only were the vegetables nutritious, the roughage helped her digestive system and her intestinal tract. She also knew not to eat fruits and vegetables at the same meal because they didn't digest well together.

Water was to be at room temperature and taken in either before or after a meal. People that use water to get their food down can't digest it as well because the water dilutes the digestive enzymes from the saliva.

CONSTIPATION

Joy had a tendency to hold her abdomen muscles tight which put a burden on her digestive system. Sometimes she didn't drink enough water, either. She knew that when she was under stress her digestive system became ineffective and she would become constipated.

So Joy took a psyllium seed mixture that she bought at the health food store to keep her colon clean and not let toxins or cholesterol build up in her body. She mixed a tablespoon of the psyllium seeds in a glass of water and drank the mixture. Then she drank another glass of water. She followed this routine morning and night. That way she knew she was getting enough water, combined with several other glasses she drank during the day. And she avoided constipation.

In the past, Joy ate fast and under pressure. She learned to slow down, and to count her bites at least ten times before swallowing. That way she had enough saliva collected in her mouth to aid her digestive process.

HARMONIZE FOODS FOR DIGESTION

Joy performed rituals with her food to harmonize them with her body. Before she ate, she held the palms of her hands on both sides of her plate. She gave thanks to her Higher Self for the nourishment she was about to receive and asked that the vibrations of her body and the food harmonize. As she gave thanks, the energy from her palms energized the food. As a part of her blessing, she asked that her body take in only what was good for it and discard the remainder. Small, more frequent meals, seemed to suit her better.

Joy knew from years of having panic attacks never to eat when she was upset. If she did, the food didn't digest and laid in her stomach like a dead stone. Now, before she ate, Joy adjusted her mind set to peace, calm, and happiness. She looked to meal times as a sacred experience where she connected with the source of life, blending higher spiritual energies with her earthly food.

Since Joy once had problems with her digestive tract, she also found other techniques to help her. One technique was an old Chinese method of rubbing or patting for five minutes around the navel in a clockwise fashion. She liked to do this at bedtime. It apparently worked for her in adjusting and realigning her energies.

Everyone has their own, unique, system. What may work well for one person may not have the same effect on another. The best way to discover what is best for you, is to experiment by adding new foods to your diet, one at a time. If a particular food makes you feel better, then continue eating it. If it makes you feel worse, then discontinue.

HERBS

Eventually, Joy tired of contributing to doctors and drug companies' retirement funds, and learned how to help herself by using natural herbs instead of synthetic drugs. She found herbs less expensive and more effective. The herbs stimulated her body to heal itself instead of masking symptoms. The naturalness of herbs made them easy for her body to digest and assimilate. Herbs have been used for natural healing for over twenty-five centuries.

The body can heal itself. Many people have found herbs, minerals and vitamins help balance and promote healing in the body. The following herbs have been found helpful in reducing panic attacks. For best results, consult a nutritionist or herbalist to determine what is right for you.

BLESSED THISTLE

Blessed Thistle strengthens the heart and lungs, and takes oxygen to the brain. It treats depression, loss of memory, nervousness and suicidal tendencies.

BLUE VERVAIN

Blue Vervain is used as a natural tranquilizer, and is an antiperiodic for all nervous problems. It has the ability to promote sweating and relaxation, allay fevers, settle stomachs and produce an overall feeling of well being. Blue Vervain contains vitamin C and small amounts of vitamin E, calcium and manganese.

CALCIUM AND MAGNESIUM

Calcium and magnesium are the "all time" mineral sedatives. Stress depletes calcium. Calcium and magnesium work together in a dialogue between the nerves and the muscles. The partnership helps the body maintain a relaxed state.

Panic attack victims are frequently found to be deficient in magnesium. One doctor maintains he can cure many patients simply by prescribing magnesium. Lack of magnesium can also cause alterations in the heart.

CATNIP

Catnip has been called nature's "Alka-Seltzer." It is used as a sedative for the nervous system. It helps in fatigue and improves circulation.

Catnip is high in vitamins A and C, and the B-complex vitamins. It contains magnesium, manganese, phosphorus, sodium, and has a trace of sulphur.

It calms the nerves during nicotine withdrawal, stress, spasms, nervous headaches, drug withdrawal, digestion, and convulsions. It also improves circulation.

GARLIC

Joy had developed high blood pressure as a result of her panic attacks. She found that taking high blood pressure medication had side effects, including depression. Then she discovered garlic. Garlic has the distinct ability to regulate blood pressure. If the pressure is low, it raises it. If the pressure is high, it lowers it. Garlic has many other legendary healing features, including:

- attacks everything that is harmful to the body
- stimulates circulation
- fights infections from bacteria and viruses
- lowers cholesterol and triglycerides
- regulates blood pressure
- wards off strokes
- inhibits cancer
- heals wounds
- promotes overall health

Laboratory and clinical tests in the last three decades have proven these claims true. It takes between one half and two full cloves of garlic a day to reap the rewards which have been noted since 4,000 B.C.

Garlic is known as *Russian penicillin.* Experts recommend eating it in both raw and cooked forms to be sure you're obtaining its full range of benefits.

Joy found that when she ate garlic chopped up in her meals, she didn't have as much of a problem with "garlic breath" as when she ate it alone. She also found the combination of garlic and cayenne pepper worked well together in reducing her blood pressure.

GOTU KOLA

Gotu Kola is called *food for the brain* because it has an energizing effect on the cells of the brain. It combats stress and improves reflexes.

Gotu Kola contains vitamins A, G and K and is high in magnesium. The uses for Gotu Kola include:

- mental problems
- high blood pressure
- energy
- brain food
- depression
- mental fatigue
- longevity
- heart strengthening
- improve memory
- the prevention of nervous breakdown
- mental and physical power
- senility

HOPS

Hops, a major natural ingredient in beer, has been in use for centuries as a calming herb. It works at soothing and nourishing the nervous system. It is good for insomnia, restlessness and shock. It decreases the desire for alcohol, and soothes, calms, relieves pain and reduces fever.

KELP

Kelp is a good promoter of glandular health. It controls the thyroid and regulates the metabolism which helps digest food. Kelp has the reputation of speeding up the burning of excess calories. Because of its ability to stimulate metabolism it is helpful in the nourishment of the body and has a beneficial effect on many disorders. It is known as the sustainer to the nervous system and the brain because it helps the brain to function normally.

Kelp contains nearly thirty minerals, all considered vital to health. It is rich in:

iodine	calcium	sulphur
silicon	lecithin	phosphorus
iron	sodium	potassium
magnesium	chlorine	copper
zinc	manganese	

It has a small amount of:

barium	boron	chromium
lithium	nickel	silver
titanium	vandium	aluminum
strontium	bismuth	chlorine
cobalt	gallium	tin
zirconium		

Kelp is rich in B-complex vitamins. It also contains vitamins A, C, E and G. It also contains the anti-sterility vitamin S, and it has anti-hemorrhage vitamin K. It works on the adrenal gland, cleans the arteries, and relieves constipation, poor digestion, and headaches.

LICORICE ROOT

Licorice Root helps with hypoglycemia, adrenal glands, stress, and helps the body make cortisone.

NIACINAMIDE

Niacinamide is another B vitamin that is extremely important as a natural tranquilizer. Since it is a vasodilator, it opens up the arteries and allows more blood to flow to the muscles, glands and organs, especially the heart. An ample supply of blood loaded with nutrients, is the very best thing for someone dealing with a stressful or tension producing situation.

PASSION FLOWER

Passion Flower is a sedative, used for menopause, headaches, neuralgia, hysteria and hypertension caused by mental attitude.

SAGE

Sage is beneficial for mental exhaustion, strengthening memory and the ability to concentrate. Sage contains:

- vitamin A
- vitamin C
- vitamin B

It also has calcium, phosphorus, sodium, and a trace of sulphur. It is helpful for:

- nerves
- stress
- nervous headaches
- digestion
- circulation
- nicotine withdrawal
- spasms
- drug withdrawal
- convulsions

SKULLCAP

Skullcap is another herb that is known as a central nervous system relaxant. It cleans and helps rebuild spinal nerves. It is called food for the nerves, supporting and strengthening them as it gives relief of chronic and acute diseases related to nervous afflictions and debility. Skullcap encourages the production of natural endorphins.

Skullcap is high in calcium, potassium, and magnesium. It also contains vitamins C, E, iron and zinc. It works primarily on the central nervous system. Its uses include helping with:

- worry
- migraines / epilepsy
- hysteria
- emotional problem
- blood pressure
- insomnia

- tremors
- alcoholism
- aches
- headaches
- tic syndrome
- twitching sensations

ST. JOHNSWORT

The herb, St. Johnswort, is used for healing wounds, depression and mild pains in the stomach, intestines and gall bladder. It is effective in headaches with excitability, hysteria, neuralgia, and menopausal symptoms, such as brain-lag, or heavy feeling in the head, or with throbbing on top of the head.

VALERIAN ROOT

Valerian root contains valepotriates. These are biochemical constituents that have very powerful sedative, anticonvulsive, hypotensive, tranquilizing, and antiaggressive properties. Valerian is recommended for short-term use. Prolonged or excessive use can cause mental depression. Rich in magnesium, potassium, copper, and some lead and zinc, it is the root herb from which the drug valium is derived. Valerian is not recommended for small children. It is used for dealing with:

- pain
- alcoholism
- drug addiction
- hypochondria
- shock
- insomnia
- ulcers
- high blood pressure
- hysteria
- palpitations
- spasms
- despondency

VITAMIN B6

Vitamin B6 is widely used for the positive effect it has on nerve health. It also works to regulate fluids in the body and reduces the pressure that might result from hypertension and accumulated water.

COMBINATIONS OF HERBS

Taking a combination of herbs, minerals and vitamins is better than taking each individually because of the synergistic effect. Then you only have to take a couple of capsules at mealtimes instead of eight to ten capsules.

Consult a herbalist to find out which combination is best for you. The benefit of these types of natural herbal tranquilizers is that they are not habit forming. Herbs can be found individually in your local health food store or they may be packaged in a combination formula, which is usually best for their synergistic formulation.

Synergism means that when you add up all the parts, the total effect is greater than the sum of the individual parts. Combining herbs allows you to get the most *healing benefits* from the least number of tablets, and the least money. Look for a formula that contains many of the herbs you want to take. The best way to work with combinations would be to take two capsules at each meal. If there is a great deal of tension in your life, then take two capsules every two hours for the first three days.

If you are also taking prescription drugs, then it is best not to take the herb at the same time. Be sure and consult your doctor before taking herbs if you are on prescribed drugs. Herbs are food, not drugs. Mixing herbs has less of a side effect than eating different foods together.

TEAS

Teas such as Chamomile help to calm the nerves and revitalize the body. Chamomile stimulates the circulation in the hands and feet. Rosehips tea perks you up, and when taken before bed, helps facilitates sound sleep. The high amount of vitamin C in rosehips helps calm and soothe the nerves. Sage tea helps to revitalize the brain and improve concentration. Sage supplies oxygen to the cortex of the brain. Use one teaspoon sage to one cup boiling water and steep three to five minutes and drink.

RESTORING HEALTH

When herbs are used for restoring health, recommended dosages are five-to-seven times that required for maintaining health. Depending on the severity of your symptoms, approximately three months of sustained high dosage is usually needed before the body is repaired. Sometimes it takes a full year for reparation to occur so that a person goes through all four seasons. The rule of thumb is that it takes one month for every year of illness to rebuild your body.

If you experience any discomfort taking an herbal combination, it may be that you are allergic to one of them. In that case stop taking the combination immediately.

It may take longer to achieve results using herbs rather than drugs, but the benefits last longer with fewer setbacks. Herbs do not mask systems like drugs do. They allow you to calm down but still identify problems you need to work through.

GLANDS

If you have panic attacks, your glands may be under pressure and not working efficiently. The following conditions may indicate that the thyroid is underfunctioning: feeling cold all the time, low energy, poor growth, and arrhythmic heartbeat. Dulse is the best thyroid stimulant, and should be taken every day to insure proper functioning of this gland. Use dulse instead of salt in soups, cereals, and whenever liquids are being cooked. One-half to one teaspoon dulse, taken daily, will sufficiently feed the thyroid and help insure vitality and normal growth.

Kelp, parsley, watercress, and Irish moss is a good synergistic complex to supplement the thyroid. Ginger root stimulates the thyroid as well and tastes delicious in salads, mustards and relishes. Mushrooms are also helpful for all conditions of the thyroid, and can be used in salads and in cooking.

Protein foods help to stimulate the adrenal system. Seeds, nuts, lentils and beans are good sources of protein.

To restore hormonal balances, eliminate from the diet all white flours, sugars, and processed foods. The best diet consists of raw fruits and lightly steamed vegetables (taken separately). To cleanse the glands, eat nothing but watermelon for one day.

FASTING

Fasting on distilled water and lemon juice is also helpful to cleanse the system. Start by doing a one day fast and use psyllium seed to help elimination. The next week, fast for two days, and the third week fast for three days and stop. Wait until the season changes and do another one day fast. Then you might fast whenever the season changes to cleanse and purify the system. A one day fast simply clears the system. A two day fast draws impurities out from the cells, and a three day fast cleanses on a cellular level.

Your cells retain the memory of everything that has ever happened to you, mentally, physically, emotionally, and spiritually. When you cleanse on the cellular level, you start clearing out things which happened in your most recent past. As you proceed in cleansing, you go back in time, all the way to the beginning. To truly cleanse takes years.

NATUROPATHIC PHILOSOPHY

One of the basic principles of the Naturopathic Philosophy is that *if a disease process and its waste products are removed from the body, it's as if that person had never experienced the disease at all.* From this standpoint, elimination is a most important process.

As you proceed toward health, you may experience what is known as a *healing crisis.* This is a state where the body throws off the rubbish it had grown used to and accommodated before. While you are in the crisis, you might feel very sick, cold, sad, and need to rest. Occasionally a *healing crisis* can take up to several days. When it is over you feel better, and your body and mind realign in a stronger fashion. Healing crisis are very beneficial.

A *healing crisis* can also involve healing emotional, spiritual, or mental trauma. Whenever you fast, ask your Higher Self for a *healing.*

Most people wait and get sick before they see a doctor. Herbs and fastings are designed to keep you in health. Have an educational consultation with a professional herbalist to determine what best suits your needs. Herbs provide the right environment for the body to balance and heal itself.

CHAPTER 18

THE HEALING POWERS

Sally swore angrily as she took the blood pressure cuff off her arm. The instrument read 160 over 99. "That's high blood pressure. It's not enough that I have panic attacks, now I develop high blood pressure along with all my other problems. Well, it's not going to get me," she swore.

"First, see your doctor, get his or her advice and have tests run. Find out what's causing the high blood pressure. Then, take some anti-stress measures on your own," I said.

"I don't want to take medicine." Sally sprang up from her chair and paced nervously around my office in her faded blue jeans and tennis shoes, absentmindedly bumping into a chair. She had a tendency to get scattered in her thinking because of her high level of anxiety.

"Take a walk in the woods beside a stream. See if that helps. Get your mind off your troubles and enjoy nature."

"That's all? It seems so simple," Sally said.

"Take your blood pressure before you go on your nature hike, and after you return. Monitor it. If it goes down, then you know communing with nature is helpful to you," I said.

The following session, Sally chattered with excitement about her week. "And you know what? My blood pressure went down at least twenty points, and some days it even went down thirty points after I walked by that little creek. It's amazing. I saw birds, and a turtle and wild flowers. Best of all, my mind cleared and I can think through things instead of guessing at answers. A lot of my panicky feelings disappeared since I started daily walks on the nature trail."

You, too, can find moments of peace and great inspiration walking in the woods, beholding a beautiful waterfall or mountain scenery. Pain, negativity and fear seem to float away in these instances, and a new vibration of freedom, hope and tranquillity emerge.

Your environment plays an important role in how you feel. For example, when you feel distraught and panicky over something, a walk beside a running stream may replace that with a sense of calmness. Try it.

NEGATIVE IONS

An increase in negative ionization of the air (the "charged" air found on mountain tops, near waterfalls, water, during thunderstorms, or at the sea) can change the chemical composition of the body's neurotransmitters. Negative ions release negativity and elevate mood. That is why you feel exhilarated when in the mountains.

NATURE

Nature walks among trees, wild flowers and beside babbling brooks, help balance your energies and restore a sense of peace. When you're trying to sort things out, a commune with nature may free your mind from stress. That makes it easier to put things in their proper perspective.

Communing with nature is a meditation. It helps you learn awareness and concentration. It also puts you in touch with a power higher than your own, giving you peace and serenity.

Talk to the flowers and trees. Put your arms around them and feel their energy. When you see a divine essence in all living things, you make connections that are very healing. Creating a oneness with the divine allows you to realize your own divinity—your common bond with all life forms.

When this attitude becomes a part of you, things seem less urgent. You may become more accepting and less perfectionistic, leaving the *shoulds*, *musts* and *oughts* behind. For example, when you look at a large tree, you can think, "Yes, I can take things one day at a time." There is no need to feel rushed and hurried, or have pressure build up. You can grow and evolve in your consciousness as you are ready.

The roots of panic attacks usually involve thoughts like, "I can't handle this," or "I'm out of control." When you commune with nature and become one with nature's healing vibrations, you know all life energy contains a balance.

Nature contains the balance between sunlight, water, soil, and nutrients. Your life contains a balance between your environment, work, play, the food you eat, sleep, family, friends, love, spirituality, the thoughts you think and the actions you set in motion.

On what do you spend time and energy? Is your life out of balance? If it is, bring it back into harmony by adjusting the time and energy you give to certain areas of your life. When you see your life as part of a larger picture, some of the urgency of everyday problems evaporates. Connecting with an image larger than yourself is one way to do this.

There are many ways to reach great inspiration and find a connection with something larger than yourself. When you let go of your personal mundane world, you can reach supreme ecstasy and heal inner fears and worries. Beholding nature is one way. Enjoy the simple pleasures of hearing a babbling brook, the feeling of tree bark touch your skin, and seeing the rainbow of colors in the grasses, flowers, and sky. Feel and sense the shapes and energy of stones, the ripples in a lake, and the surge of the ocean tide.

Take advantage of the joys and gifts in nature, for these continuously help to balance and harmonize you. Appreciate them.

MUSIC

Music can help balance and increase your harmony with life. It has been used as part of the healing process since ancient times. Music, wisely used, can:

- alter the heartbeat and affect the nervous system favorably
- promote greater relaxation and flexibility in accepting new attitudes
- bring clearance and purification to the body
- emotions and personality thinking patterns increase
- physical vitality; relieve fatigue and inertia
- pierce through anxiety and tensions, and uplift feelings
- focus thinking, clarify goals, promote courage and follow-through
- stimulate creativity and sensitivity
- expand your consciousness of God and spiritual attunement

Great music helps balance and integrate the different aspects of your personality. It cannot, however, enter you and revitalize you if you are distracted or poorly prepared. Take time to prepare yourself for your music. Then it can play through you, not just around you. You receive the full power and beauty of great music by relaxing, and linking with the melodies you are hearing. To get the best benefits from your music:

- Take a comfortable position in a chair or lie on the floor.
- If you are outside, you may want to find a shady spot and lean against a tree.
- Become quiet and talk to yourself.
- Tell your body to relax, your thoughts to calm and your feelings to subside.
- Surrender to the music.
- Release your tensions into the music.
- Feel the music pulling the negativity and turmoil out of you.
- Breathe in the music, let go completely and travel into the sound.

- Take time to absorb the music.
- After the piece has finished, sit quietly for a few minutes.

Music is best enjoyed in a beautiful environment. But its benefits are not lost if you play great music while you're doing your chores or working.

While music can energize and inspire you, different musical works appeal specifically to certain areas. Some music primarily affects the physical body. These pieces give strength and energy. Other selections influence your feelings and emotions. Still other selections appeal to your mind, inspiring you with new ideas and creativity. There is also music that speaks directly to your heart and soul.

The physical body responds to the heavy sounds of bass notes, brass, and the percussion found in marches. Brass pierces through inertia and negativity. Marches awaken loyalty and are often a powerful medicine for combating an enemy, either external or within yourself.

Music to Activate Your Physical Body

Overtures and movie soundtracks vitalize you with their strong frequencies. They are very powerful and one of these at a time is enough. Most of the following selections are very strong, so absorb the power before playing more of this kind of music.

Pomp and Circumstance, No. 1, - Sir Edward Elgar
Triumphal March (from Aida) - Giuseppe Verdi
Stars and Stripes Forever - John Phillip Sousa
Die Meistersinger - Wagner
Die Fledermaus - J. Strauss
Don Giovanni; Magic Flute - Mozart
Dances With Wolves

Born Free
Star Wars

Music for Strained Emotions

The woodwinds and stringed instruments effect your feelings and moods. The key to a healthy emotional nature is to express your feelings; not repress them. Balancing your emotions takes time, especially if you repress your feelings.

You can release emotions creatively and clear out emotional blockages through woodwind music. The following selections are wonderful for strained emotions:

Debussy - Clair de lune
Rachmaninoff - Second Symphony

Music to Help Release Anger

When you hear music, you may feel emotional negativity and tension drain away. Some music not only absorbs the energies you release, it carries you into higher states of consciousness. The following selections illustrate this concept:

Beethoven - Egmont Overture
Tchaikovsky - Symphony No. 5 (last movement)
Wagner - Ride of the Valkyries

Music to Calm and Rebalance Anger, Hurt and Pain

Bach, J.S. - Two Concertos for Two Pianos
Handel - Harp Concerto
Dexter - Golden Voyage I

Music to Pierce Through Depression, Fears and Doubt

Beethoven - Piano Concerto No. 5
Dvorak - Symphony No. 8

Mozart - Symphony No. 35

Mendelssohn - Symphony No. 4

Rachmaninoff - Piano Concerto No. 2 (final movement)

Music for Strength and Courage

Battle Hymn of the Republic

Elgar - Pomp and Circumstances March, No. 1

Music to Relax and Unwind

Wagner - Evening Star (from Tannhauser)

Halpern-Kelly - Ancient Echoes

Music for Clear Thinking

The string instruments appeal to the mind. They help you find mental clarity. Your attitudes effect what happens to you and the kind of day you have. Music pleasing to the mind is clear melodically and rhythmically. Music from the Baroque period is melodic and rhythmic. Such music helps your mind to focus.

Examples are:

Brahms - Violin Concerto

Handel - Water Music

Baroque string music of Telemann, Vivaldi, Albinoni, Corelli, Torelli, and others.

Music for Meditation and Prayer

The greatest, most inspiring music speaks to your soul. The soul is attuned by the harp and organ, wind chimes, and high strings. This type of music releases negativity and heaviness and sends you back into the world with renewed hope and vigor.

Use music to prepare you for meditation. Music stills your body, emotions and mind, so your soul can speak to you. An effective affirmation is "The music of the heavens moves through me." Keep a notebook handy to jot down the impressions you receive. Ask yourself, "What feelings does the music awaken in me?" "In what body parts do I feel the music most?"

Where you feel the music is a signal that either more energy is needed in this area, or that diffusing the energy is most needed. Music serves as a balancing device and helps harmonize your system. When the music is over, give thanks for the good the music has brought you. The following selections may be used in preparing for meditation:

Paul Horn - Inside the Taj Mahal

Handel - Largo (from Xerxes)

Wagner - Prelude to Act 1 (from Lohengrin)

Mozart - Vesperae Solennes de Confessore (Sanctur)

Faur'e - In Paradise (from Requiem)

Find the kind of music you need to balance, awaken, release and refine your emotions. Keep these favorites near you. Sing their melodies and let them vibrate through you.

FINE ARTS

Fine art is another medium to find inspiration and connect with images larger than yourself. At the theater, the stage actors and the audience connect. The experience of the drama, and the experience of the actors creating it is invisible. If you are in the audience, you connect with the essence of what's being portrayed and become more open.

When you see a great painting, play, or any fine art, you connect with levels that reach higher than the physical. As you capture the moment, a profound sense emerges of a larger vision and dimension of yourself. These experiences allow you to put stress and panic attacks into perspective and see yourself as more than your problems.

LAUGHTER

Whatever helps break up negative perceptions, fears and worries and replaces those energies with positive perceptions, heals. *Laughter is the best medicine.* Laughter shifts your internal chemistry and profoundly impacts the body's systems, including the nervous, circulatory, endocrine, and immune systems.

Laughter takes your mind off your troubles. It helps you focus outward to the world, instead of drawing into a personal world of woes.

Physically, laughter effects most, if not all, of the major physiologic systems of the body. The cardiovascular system gets exercised as your heart rate and blood pressure rise and fall. Your respiratory system gets a workout as the vigorous air exchanges in your lungs. Your muscles release tension. Opiates may be released into your blood system, creating the same feelings that long-distance joggers experience as "runner's high." Laughter is often called "inner jogging" because every system gets a good workout.

Humor can be a form of relief. You might laugh when you feel you have escaped a great danger. Make a list of things that are humorous to you. You may be surprised with what you compile. Sometimes people even find humor in economic difficulties, death, alcoholism and extremes of behavior.

A good sense of humor is your first line of defense against the pain and unpleasantness you experience in life. It allows you to appreciate ludicrous events and ideas.

Humor loosens you up. A sense of humor is more than the ability to laugh. Many people have nervous laughter. That is not humor. You might laugh when you feel happy. But the best way to use humor is to develop the ability to laugh at yourself. It takes courage and intelligence to recognize your own foolishness. When you use humor in this way, it becomes a coping skill. Humor gives you power and a new perspective. It presents you with alternative views of your situation and helps keep you in balance. If you can find humor in something, you can survive it; even a panic attack.

CHAPTER 19

SELF-ESTEEM

"My life has come to this," Connie wept in despair. Her curly, brown, hair fell softly around her face. "I started using prescription drugs to stop my panic attacks. But, it didn't stop there. I was hooked the first time I took a pill. It made me feel good. So I took two instead of one. Then I took three and four to feel even better—or not feel at all." Connie relaxed, leaned back in the therapy chair and looked at the ceiling.

"You see," Connie poured out her life story, "I've always felt bad about myself. I spent my whole childhood miserably depressed. When I grew up and got on my own, I was scared to be alone. I felt I needed protection. I did need protection when I was little, protection from my stepfather. He was always trying to stick his hands down my panties." She clasped her hands over her crotch as if still trying to protect herself.

"Then, after I was grown, I started having panic attacks. My life was out of control. I took drugs to escape the way I felt. I discovered that when I took too many pills, I numbed out my feelings. It didn't take long to figure out I could go to different doctors and make up symptoms and get all kinds of prescriptions. I started mixing the pills together to get a high. At first I thought I'd die, but when I didn't, I took more. For six years I went around like a zombie. Finally, in desperation, I slashed my wrists. When I woke up in the hospital, I was furious I was still alive," she cried.

Connie's choices in life had been narrowed to which pills to take each day. Her self-esteem was extremely low.

SELF-ESTEEM

Self-esteem reflects the way you feel about yourself—your self-image. The more helpless and out of control you feel, the lower your self-esteem. Bolstering your self-esteem by using another person, relationship, drugs or alcohol, a job, or living in the "right" neighborhood, doesn't work. Self-esteem is internal. It involves all the various aspects of your being:

- your ability to accept yourself as you are
- your ability to establish relationships

- your ability to develop independence
- your ability to care and nurture yourself physically, emotionally, mentally and spiritually
- your ability to provide financial security for yourself and your children
- your ability to develop your creativity
- your ability to accomplish your goals
- your ability to have a sense of belonging to a group
- your ability to assert yourself
- your ability to have control over your life
- your ability to set limits and boundaries with others
- your ability to have an intimate relationship
- your ability to make intelligent choices for your life

Nothing deflates your self-esteem faster than your own criticism. When you look into the mirror, you place a value upon what you see. You may like what you see, and think, "Gee, I look great." Or, you may pick at yourself, thinking, "I'm too fat, my hair is awful looking and my face is sagging." It's this latter type of critical thinking that's disastrous to your self-esteem. You wouldn't say those things to another person yet, when you're critical of yourself, you sabotage your self-esteem.

If you don't assert yourself, you're vulnerable to others taking advantage of you. When they do, your self-esteem sinks. This starts a vicious cycle of feeling worthless.

Women who stay in abusive relationships eventually think less and less of themselves. They feel devalued as human beings—until the abuse stops and they receive treatment. Not standing up for yourself isn't all that causes low self-esteem. The way you are reared impacts directly on how you feel about yourself.

Abused children—physically, mentally, emotionally, sexually—often justify the abuse. Parents are "right" in the child's mind. So they reason they deserve what happens when they are abused.

This serves several purposes. First, if the parents are right in abusing "bad children," the children imagine in some magical way they can become "good" and stop the abuse. Second, if the child perceives the parents are "good," the parents will continue to care for them, thereby insuring survival.

But abuse isn't the only way self-esteem is negatively effected. Excessively critical parents make you feel, "you're never good enough."

Ironically, after you grow up, you constantly strive for perfection, feeling inferior all the while. You whip yourself mentally with criticism. You treat yourself as your parents did, and abuse yourself. The result is that you never accept yourself. You may try to prove your worthiness by attaining numerous achievements, rather than simply accepting who you are.

People from homes where their parents abused alcohol or drugs feel insecure because of the chaos they lived in. They are unable to trust others because their parents were so unreliable. Even if only one parent abuses alcohol, the remaining parent is usually so preoccupied with the problems caused by the alcoholism that the children are never given focused attention. The result is confusion. The children then suffer in developing a positive identity. Their identity is usually based on the feeling of loss.

If you suffered a major loss or trauma in your childhood and no one was really "there" for you, you may feel abandoned. This results in feelings of worthlessness and emptiness. After you're grown, the resulting despair is often filled by addictions to people, work, or alcohol—trying to become whole. But instead of feeling better, you're left feeling even worse, with your self-esteem on a downward spiral.

Some parents reject their children, either by neglect or by imparting them with a feeling that they are unwanted. This damaging attitude teaches them to grow up doubting their very right to exist. If this was your situation, you may identify with the way you thought your parents felt about you. If you felt unloved, you may judge yourself unworthy and hate yourself. You may persecute yourself, use self-sabotage, self-destructive behavior and become self-rejecting.

The better your childhood experiences, the more self-reliant and confident you are. One of the basic ingredients of your self-esteem is your perception of your own worth in the eyes of your parents or parental figures. Among the many factors in child rearing that lead to a healthy self-esteem, the most significant is where the parents reward the child's self-accomplishments.

INNER CHILD WORK

It is never too late to have a happy childhood. Even though you can't change the past, you can do many things to change how you feel. Reparenting your inner child can provide corrective emotional experiences. Aspects of your personality fragmented due to emotional trauma or loss, can be healed and integrated. Accomplished over a period of a year or longer, inner child work may totally restructure your personality.

To begin your inner child work, relax and close your eyes. Go to your safe place as described in Chapter 12. Visualize yourself with all your adult strengths. Focus your awareness on any internal pain or fear you may feel. Picture those feelings as a hurt child. You might use an old photograph as a reminder. Go to your inner child, and make friends. Tell your inner child you're here from the future, and assure your younger self that he or she survived. Ask your inner child to tell you about the fear or pain.

Then, tell your inner child you're here to protect him or her, and to make sure he or she never has to go through that again. Visualize your inner child on your lap or knee. Hug the child and tell your younger self he or she is loved and wanted. Ask, "What can I do to help you?" "What do you need from me at this time?"

When you are finished reassuring your inner child, play with your inner child and have some fun. When you are ready to close your time with your inner child and return to your outer reality, tell your child you will come back again. When you leave visualize your inner child in a safe place. Make an appointment for another time and be certain to keep it.

Write letters to your inner child. Another method, previously described, is to write to your inner child using your dominant hand.

Your inner child will answer by writing with your non-dominant hand. You could also write a letter to your parents with your non-dominant hand telling them all the things you needed from them but didn't get. Then start giving yourself those things and meeting those unmet needs from the past.

Anytime you experience a negative feeling state, you can take this as a plea from your inner child for attention. Close your eyes and ask your inner child what he or she is trying to tell you. Then comfort the child and realize what that does for your feelings.

Repeat your inner child work often. Each time you may see many different aspects of yourself. Comfort your inner child, and accept the pain and anger the child has not been allowed to express.

You become your own parent as you do the inner child work. Your unconscious accepts what you do as a part of your total reality. The purpose of reworking the past is to release it.

Don't stop there. Continue to work with your inner child, providing experiences you never had. Visualize your inner child at the zoo, have birthday parties, and help him or her with schoolwork. Be there for your child. Teach you inner child to trust in life. Help your inner child believe that life is self-affirming. In this way, you build a foundation based on confidence and security.

Judy, age thirty-two, had intense panic attacks. She had been treated with drugs and she used them to overmedicate herself. Her central nervous system cord, as it appeared in her visualizations, looked like frayed wiring.

She shook constantly and was extremely depressed. Judy's first step was to learn how to relax. After learning progressive relaxation and biofeedback, she let herself go into a deep state of relaxation. She saw herself as a young child running and playing in a stream, splashing water and having fun—which she had never done before.

Judy realized, after she came out of the relaxation, she didn't take any time for herself. She had grown up duty-bound, taking care of her alcoholic father. She had extended this pattern, after she grew up, to taking care of others. She felt her panic attacks were a message, telling her that she denied her own needs. Her real self was trying to break through, telling her to take time for herself.

Judy visualized her central nervous system healed, her inner child playing and laughing, saying "No" to her deceased father and refusing to take care of him.

She used spiritual reparenting affirmations to release the tension and anger at not getting her needs met in childhood. Her self-esteem heightened, and, several weeks later, Judy reported having sexual feelings and being orgasmic for the first time in her life.

SPIRITUAL AFFIRMATIONS

Spiritual affirmations to release parental neglect and abuses include:

- I release my belief, perception and judgment that my father/mother failed to hold me, hug me, and love me every day until I was five years old.
- I release my belief, perception, and judgment that my father/mother failed to hold me, hug me, love, and praise me every day until I was ten.
- I release my belief, perception, and judgment that my father/mother failed to hold me, hug me, love me, and tell me how wonderful I was every day until I was fifteen.
- I release my belief, perception, and judgment that my father/ mother failed to hold me, hug me, love me, and confirm me every day until I was twenty.
- I release my belief, perception, and judgment that my father/mother failed to hold me, hug me, and praise me every day of my life.
- I release my belief, perception, and judgment that my father/mother failed me any time I needed him/her to hold me, hug me, love me, praise me, care for me, confirm me and tell me how wonderful I am.

Spiritual affirmations and reparenting with inner child work are especially effective for heightening self-esteem. So is being in therapy or attending a support group. The positive regard your therapist has for you, helps you feel better about yourself as well as resolve conflicts.

Practicing assertiveness also contributes to positive self-esteem. According to researchers using before and after tests, assertiveness training greatly increases self-esteem. No matter how low your present self-esteem, you can raise it by working on your assertiveness.

Positive affirmations such as "I am a worthwhile person" and "I love myself" are always helpful in raising your self-esteem. You can also talk to the child within by saying, "You are lovable."

TAKE ACTION

The most important thing you can do to raise your self-esteem is to *take action.* Act instead of react. Do those things that are positive and meaningful for you. Give yourself the nurturing, consistency, discipline and affection you never received. Help yourself overcome a lifetime of insecurity. Develop the ability to give to yourself what your parents could not. Think through your decisions to logical conclusions. In this way, you learn to trust yourself. When mistakes happen, use them as learning experiences.

As you venture forth, trust in life. Trust in things which are life affirming. Take care of yourself, nurture yourself and find ways to meet your basic human needs. Self-esteem is dependent on recognizing and taking care of all your needs. In this way, you focus away from fear and doubt, and rob panic of its power over you.

Bibliography

Books

Allison, Audle. *Meditation*, The Lotus Center, Ok. City, Ok. 1975.

Assagiolio, Roberto. *Pyschosynthesis*, Penguin Books, N. Y., 1965.

Babior, Shirley; Goldman, Carol. *Overcoming Panic Attacks*, CompCare Publishers, Minneapolis, 1983.

Bandler, Richard; Grinder, John. *Frogs Into Princes*, Real People Press, Moab, Utah, 1979.

Bandler, Richard; Grinder, John. *Trance-formations*, Real People Press, Moab, Utah, 1981.

Benson, Gerbert. *The Relaxation Response,* Avon Books, N. Y., 1975.

Benson, Herbert. *Your Maximum Mind,* Avon Books, N. Y., 1987.

Borysenko, Joan. *Guilt Is The Teacher, Love Is The Lesson,* Warner Books, Inc., N. Y., 1990.

Borysenko, Joan. *Minding The Body, Mending The Mind,* Bantam Books, N. Y., 1987.

Bourne, Edmound J. *The Anxiety And Phobia Workbook,* New Harbinger Publications, Inc., Oakland, Ca., 1990.

Bradshaw, John. *Healing The Shame That Binds You,* Health Communications, Deerfield Beach, Fl., 1988.

Bradshaw, John. *Homecoming*, Bantam Books, N Y., 1990.

Branden, Nathaniel. *Honoring The Self,* Bantam Books, N. Y., 1983.

Branden, Nathaniel. *How To Raise Your Self-Esteem,* Bantam Books, N. Y., 1987.

Burns, David. *Feeling Good,* Signet, N. Y., 1980.

Campbell, Don G. *Introduction To The Musical Brain,* Magnamusic-Baton, Inc., 1983.

Campbell, Peter A.; McMahon, Edwin M.. *Bio-Spirituality,* Loyola University Press, Chicago, 1985.

Charlesworth, Edward; Nathan, Ronald. *Stress Management,* Ballanatine, N. Y., 1982.

Clum, George A. *Coping With Panic*, Brooks/Cole Publishing Company, Pacific Grove, Ca., 1990.

Davis, Martha; Eshelman, Elizabeth Robbins; McKay, Mathew. *The Relaxation And Stress Reduction Workbook,* New Harbinger Publications, Inc., Oakland, Ca., 1988.

Fishel, Ruth. *The Journey Within,* Health Communications, Inc., Deerfield Beach, Fl., 1987.

Friel, John; Friel, Linda. *Adult Children,* Health Communications, Inc., Deerfield Beeach, Fl., 1988.

Gawain, Shakti. *Creative Visualization,* Bantam Books, N.Y., 1979.

____. *Reflections In the Light,* New World Library, San Rafael, Ca., 1988.

Gendlin, Eugene. *Focusing,* Bantam Books, N. Y., 1981.

Gold, Mark S.. *The Good News About Panic, Anxiety, and Phobias,* Bantam Books, N. Y., 1989.

Gordon, David; Meyers-Anderson, Maribeth. *Phoenix*, Meta Publications, Cupertino, Ca., 1981.

Hall, Dorothy. *Creating Your Herbal Profile,* Keats Publishing, Inc., New Canna, Conn., 1988.

Handly, Robert; Neff, Pauline. *Anxiety and Panic Attacks,* Fawcett Crest, N. Y., 1985.

Hailparn M.S.; *Fear No More,* St. Martin's Press, N. Y., 1988.

Hittleman, Richard. *Introduction To Yoga*, Bantam Books, N. Y., 1969.

Houston, Jean; Masters, Robert. *Listening To The Body,* Dalacorte Press, N. Y.,1987.

Jackson, Mildren; Teague, Terri. *The Handbook For Alternatives To Chemical Medicine,* Lawton-Teague Publications, Oakland Ca., 1975.

Jones, E. Stanley. *How To Pray,* Abingdon Press, Nashville, 1943.

Kelsey, Morton T. *The Other Side Of Silence,* N.Y., 1976.

BIBLIOGRAPHY

Klein, Allen. *The Healing Power Of Humor*, Jeremy P. Tarcher, Inc., Los Angeles, 1988.

King, Serge. *Imagineering For Health,* The Theosophical Publishing House, Wheaton, Illinios, 1981.

Lerner, Harriet Goldhor. *The Dance Of Anger*, Harper and Row Publishers, N. Y., 1985.

LeShan, Edgar. *How To Meditate*, Bantam Books, N. Y., 1974.

Lingerman, Hal A. *The Healing Energies Of Music*, The Theosophical Publishing House, Wheaton, Ill., 1983.

Lowen, Alexander. *Bioenergetics,* Penquin Books, N. Y., 1975.

Lust, John. *The Herb Book,* Bantam Books, N. Y., 1974.

McKay, Matthew; Fanning, Patrick. *Self-Esteem*, New Harbinger Publications, Oakland, Cal., 1987.

Norwood, Robin. *Women Who Love Too Much,* Pocket Books, N. Y., 1985.

Odle, Chris. *Practical Visualization,* The Aquarian Press, Wellingborough, Northamptonshire, England, 1990.

Ornstein, Robert; Thompson, Richard. *The Amazing Brain,* Houghton Mifflin Company, Boston, 1984.

Peper, Erik; Ancoli, Sonia; Quinn, Michele. *Mind/Body Integration,* Plenum Press, N. Y., 1979.

Satir, Virginia. *Peoplemaking,* Science and Behavior Books, Inc., Palo Alto, Ca., 1972.

Sedlacek, Keith. *Finding The Calm Within You,* Signet, N.Y., 1989.

Segal, Jeanne. *Living Beyond Fear,* Ballantine Books, N. Y.,1984.

Sheehan, David. *The Anxiety Disease,* Bantam, N. Y., 1983.

Sontag, Susan. *Illness As Metaphor*, Farrar Straus Giroux, N. Y., 1978.

Terr, Lenore. *Too Scared To Cry,* Harper and Row Publishers, Inc., N. Y., 1990.

Viorst, Judith. *Necessary Losses,* Fawcett Gold Medal, N. Y., 1986.

Wade, Carlson. *Natural Hormones,* Parker Publishing Company, Inc., West Nyack, N. Y., 1972.

Whitfield, Charles. *Healing The Child Within,* Health Communications, Inc., Deerfield Beach, Fl., 1987.

Wilson, R. Reid. *Don't Panic,* Harper and Row Publishers, Inc., N.Y., 1986.

Articles

Beitman, Bernard; Basha, Imad M.; Trombka, Lawrence H.; Jarantna, Mahinda A.; Russel, Barbara; Flaker Greg; Anderson, Sharon. 'Pharmacoatherapeutic Treatment of Panic Disorder in Patients Presenting With Chest Pain' *The Journal of Family Practice* Vol. 28, No. 2: 177-180, (1989).

Bourdon, Karen H.; Boyd, Jeffrey H.; Rae, Donald S.; Burns, Barbara J.; Thompson James W.; Locke, Ben Z. 'Gender Differences in Phobias: Results of the ECA Community Survey' *Journal of Anxiety Disorders* Vol. 2, pp. 227-241, (1988)

Brett, Elizabeth A.; Ostroff, Robert. 'Imagery and Post-Traumatic Stress Disorder: An Overview' *American Journal of Psychiatry* 142:4, (April 1985).

Cook III, Edwin W.; Melamed, Barbara G.; Cuthbert, Bruce N.; McNeil, Daniel W.; Lang, Peter J. 'Emotional Imagery and the Differential Diagnosis of Anxiety' *Journal of Consulting and Clinical Psychology* Vol. 54, No. 5, 734-740, (1988).

Coryell, William; Endicott, Jean; Andreasen, Keller; Martin B.; Clayton, Paula J.; Hirschfeld, Robert M.A.; Scheftner, William A.; Winokur, George. 'Depression and Panic Attacks; The Significance of Overlap as Reflected in Follow-Up and Family Study Data; *American Journal of Psychiatry* 145:3, (March 1988).

Coryell, William; Noyes, Russell. 'Placebo Response in Panic Disorder' *American J. of Psychiatry* 145:9 (September 1988).

BIBLIOGRAPHY

Dattilio, Frank M. 'The Use of Paradoxical Intention in the Treatment of Panic Attacks' *Journal of Counseling and Development* Vol. 66 (October 1987).

Delamater, Ronald J.; McNamara, J. Regis. 'The Social Impact of Assertiveness' *Behavior Modification* Vol. 10 No. 2, (April 1986) 139-158.

Donnell, Christina D.; McNally, Richard J. 'Anxiety Sensitivity and History of Panic as Predictors of Response to Hyperventilation' *Behav. Res. Ther.* Vol. 27, No. 4, pp. 325-332, (1989).

Faravelli, Carol; Pallanti, Stefano. 'Recent Life Events and Panic Disorder' *American Journal of Psychiatry* 146:5, May 1989).

Gorman, Jack; Fyer, Minna:; Goetz, Raymond; Askanazi, Jeffrey. 'Ventilatory Physiology of Patients With Panic Disorder' *Arch. Gen. Psychiatry* Vol. 45, (Jan. 1988).

Green, Alyce; Green, Elmer. 'Biofeedback; Research and Therapy' *The Menninger Foundation Research Department,* Topeka, Kansas (1975).

Green, Elmer; Green, Alyce; Walters, Dale. 'Biofeedback for Mind-Body Self-Regulation: Healing and Creativity' *The Menninger Foundation Research Department,* Topeka, Kansas (October 30, 1971).

Grunhaus, Leon. 'Clinical and Psychobiological Characteristics of Simultaneous Panic Disorder and Major Depression" *American Journal of Psychiatry* 145:10, (October 1988).

Hoffman, Lee. 'Recognizing Panic Disorder' *ADAMHA News,* U.S. Department of Health and Human Services Vol. XVI No. 3 (May June 1990).

Holloway, Wendy; McNally, Richard J. 'Effects of Anxiety Sensitivity on the Response to Hyperventilation' *Journal of*

Abornmal Psychology Vol. 96, No. 4, 330-334, (1987).

Kane, Jr., Francis; J. Harper, Robert G.; Wittels, Ellison. 'Angina as a Symptom of Psychiatric Illness' *Southern Medical Journal* Vol. 81, No. 11 (1988).

Klerman, Gerald L. 'Overview of the Cross-National Collaborative Panic Study' *Arch. Gen. Psychiatry* Vol 45, (May 1988).

Kneisl, Carol. 'Healing the Wounded, Neglected Inner Child of the Past' *Nursing Clinics of North America* Vol. 26, No. 3, (September 1991).

Koksal, Falih; Power, Kevin G. 'Four Systems Anxiety Questionnaire (FSAQ); A Self-Report Measure of Somatic Cognitive, Behavioral, and Feeling Components' *Journal of Personality Assessment* 54 (3 & 4) , 534-545 (1990).

Mannuzza, Salvatore; Fyer, Abby J.; Martin, Lynn Y.; Gallops, Mark S.; Endicott, Jean; Gorman, Jack; Liebowitz, Michael R.; Klein, Donald. 'Reliability of Anxiety Assessment' *Arch. Gen. Psychiatry* Vol. 46, (December 1989).

Markowitz, Jeffrey S.; Weissman, Myrna M.; Ouellette, Robert; Lish, Jenifer D.; Klerman, Gerald L. 'Quality of Life in Panic Disorder' *Arch. Gen. Psychiatry* Vol. 46, (November 1989).

McNally, Richard J.; Lorenz, Marleen. 'Anxiety Sensitivity in Agoraphobics' *Journal Behavorial Therapy & Experimental Psychiatry* Vol. 18, No. 1. pp. 3-11, (1987).

McNally, Richard J. 'Is Anxiety Sensitivity Distinguishable From Trait Anxiety? Reply to Lilienfeld, Jacob, and Turner' *Journal of Abnormal Psychology* Vol. 98. No. 2, 193-194. (1989).

Mellman, Thomas A.; Uhde, Thomas W. 'Sleep Panic Attacks: New Clinical Findings and Theoretical Implications' *American Journal of Psychiatry* 146:9, (September 1989).

BIBLIOGRAPHY

________ 'Electroencephalographic Sleep in Panic Disorder' *Arch. General Psychiatry* Vol. 46, (February 1989).

Morrison, James K.; Becker, Robert E. 'Reduction of Anxiety: Comparative Effectiveness of Imagery Psychotherapy vs Self-Help Seminars' *Psychological Reports,* 53, 417-418, (1983).

Moreau, Donna L.; Weissman, Myrna; Warner, Virginia. 'Panic Disorder in Children at High Risk for Depression' *American Journal or Psychiatry* 146:8, (August 1989).

Orenstein, Herbert; Peskind, Arthur; Raskind, Murray A. 'Thyroid Disorders in Female Psychiatric Patients with Panic Disorder or Agoraphobia' *American Journal of Psychiatry* 145:11, (November 1988).

Peniston, Eugene; Kulkosky, Paul. 'Alcoholic Personality and Alpha-Theta Brainwave Training' *Medical Psychotherapy* Vol. 3, pp. 37-55, (1990).

________ 'Alpha-Theta Brainwave Training & B-Endorphin Levels in Alcoholics' *Alcoholism: Clinical and Experimental Research* Vol. 13, No. 2 (March-April) 1989.

Perera, Judith. 'The Hazards of Heavy Breathing' *New Scientist* (December 3, 1988).

Perrince, Stephen. 'Phobias: The Facts About Fears' *Parents* (September 1989).

Pitman, Roger K.; Forgue, Dennis F.; de Jong, Jacob B.; Caliborn, James M. 'Psychophysiologic Assessment of Post-Traumatic Stress Disorder Imagery in Vietnam Combat Veterans' *Arch. Gen. Psychiatry* Vol. 44, (Nov. 1987).

Reich, James H. 'DSM-III Personality Disorders and the Outcome of Treated Panic Disorder' *American Journal of Psychiatry* 145:9 (September 1988).

Reich, Peter. 'Panic Attacks and the Risk of Suicide' *The New England Journal of Medicine* (Nov. 2, 1989).

Reiss, Steven; Peterson, Rolf A.; Gursky, M. David.; McNally, Richard J. 'Anxiety Sensitivity, Anxiety Frequency and the Prediction of Fearfulness' *Behavioral Res. Ther.* Vol. 24, No. 1 pp. 1-8, (1986).

Rosenabaum, Jeffold F.; Biederman, Joseph; Gersten, Michael; Hirshfeld, Dina R.; Meminger, Susan R.; Herman, John B.; Kagan, Jerome; Reznaick, J. Steven; Snidman, Nancy. 'Behavioral Inhibition in Children of Parents With Panic Disorder and Agoraphobia' *Arch. Gen. Psychiatry* Vol. 45, (May 1988).

Stein, Murray B.; Schmidt, Peter J.; Rubinow, David R. 'Panic Disorder and the Menstrual Cycle; Panic Disorder Patients, Health Control Subjects, and Patients with Premenstrual Syndrome' *Am. J. Psychiatry* 146:10, (October 1989).

Stein, Murray B.; Shea, Cheryl A.; Uhde, Thomas. 'Social Phobic Symptoms in Patients With Panic Disorder: Practical and Theoretical Implications' *American Journal of Psychiatry* 146:2 (February 1989).

Stein, Murray B.; Uhde, Thomas W. 'Thyroid Indices in Panic Disorder' *American Journal of Psychiatry* 145:6, (June 1988).

______ 'Autoimmune Thyroiditis and Panic Disorder' *American Journal of Psychiatry* 146:2, (February 1989).

Stutman, Randall K.; Bliss, Eugene L. 'Post-Traumatic Stress Disorder, Hypnotizability, and Imagery' *American Journal of Psychiatry* 142:6, (June 1985).

Russell, Johnna; Kushner, Matt, Beitman, Bernard; Bartels, Kim. 'Nonfearful Panic Disorder in Neurology Patients Validated by Lactate Challenge' *American Journal of Psychiatry* 148:3, (March 1991).

Teicher, Martin H.; 'Biology of Anxiety' *Medical Clinics of North America* Vol. 72. No. 4, (July 1988).

Thompson, A.H.; Bland, R.C.; Orn, Helene T. 'Relationship and Chronology of Depression, Agoraphobia, and Panic Disorder in the General Population' *The Journal of Nervous and Mental Disease* Vol. 177, No. 8, (1989).

Tyrer, P.; Murphy S.; Kingdon, D.; Brothwell, J.; Gregory; Seivewright, N.; Ferguson, B.; Barczak, P.; Darling, C.; Johnson, A.L. 'The Nottingham Study of Neurotic Disorder: Comparison of Drug and Psychological Treatments' *The Lancet* (Saturday 30, July 1988).

Weissman, Myrna M.; Klerman, Gerald L.; Markowitz; Ouellette, Robert. 'Suicidal Ideation and Suicide Attempts in Panic Disorder and Attacks' *The New England Journal of Medicine* Vol. 321, No. 18, (November 2, 1989).

Index

A

B

INDEX

INDEX

N

O

P

Q

R

ORDER FORM

Telephone orders: (918) 488-9530

Postal Orders: STONEHORSE PRESS, P.O. BOX 701595, Tulsa, Oklahoma 74170.

Please send me ___ copies of PANIC NO MORE at $12.95 each.

Name:____

Address:____

City:_____________________ State:___________Zip_________

Sales tax:
Please add 7.5 % for books shipped to Oklahoma addresses (97 cents)

Shipping:
Please allow $1.05 for postage and surface shipping and 75 cents for each additional book
Air Mail: $3.00 per book

Payment:

__Check __ Visa, __ MasterCard

Card number______________________Exp. date:_____/_______

Name on card: ____

CALL AND ORDER NOW

ABOUT THE AUTHOR

Jean Carlton received her degree in Master of Social Work from the University of Oklahoma. She is a licensed Clinical Social Worker and psychotherapist, a certified (NLP) Neuro-Linguistic Programmer, has trained at the Jungian Institute in Switzerland and at the renowned Menninger Foundation in Topeka, Kansas. Jean Carlton is a noted lecturer, has taught at several colleges and universities, and authored numerous articles. She specializes in the treatment of anxiety, and stress-related disorders. She is in private practice in Tulsa, Oklahoma.

Questions and comments to Jean Carlton may be sent to P. O. Box 701595, Tulsa, Oklahoma 74170.

NOTES

NOTES

NOTES